THE
PILGRIM

THE PILGRIM

SAS WHO DARES WINS

COLIN MACLACHLAN

Pen & Sword
MILITARY

AN IMPRINT OF PEN & SWORD BOOKS LTD.
YORKSHIRE - PHILADELPHIA

First published in Great Britain in 2025 by
PEN AND SWORD MILITARY
An imprint of
Pen & Sword Books Limited
Yorkshire – Philadelphia

ISBN 978 1 03612 658 2

Typeset in Times New Roman 12/16 by
SJmagic DESIGN SERVICES, India.
Printed and bound in the UK by CPI Group (UK) Ltd.

The Publisher's authorised representative in the EU for product safety is
Authorised Rep Compliance Ltd., Ground Floor, 71 Lower Baggot Street,
Dublin D02 P593, Ireland.
www.arccompliance.com

For a complete list of Pen & Sword titles please contact
PEN & SWORD BOOKS LIMITED
George House, Units 12 & 13, Beevor Street, Off Pontefract Road,
Barnsley, South Yorkshire, S71 1HN, England
E-mail: enquiries@pen-and-sword.co.uk
Website: www.pen-and-sword.co.uk

or

PEN AND SWORD BOOKS
1950 Lawrence Rd, Havertown, PA 19083, USA
E-mail: uspen-and-sword@casematepublishers.com
Website: www.penandswordbooks.com

CONTENTS

FOREWORD

'There's a unique connection for people like Colin and myself. Colin is in a pretty exclusive club. He gives a good account of the operations he has been involved in and he has had his fair share of the big ones. Soldiers will recognise from his stories that sense of excitement mixed with fear and anxiety when you go into action. That takes one sort of bravery, but it takes a special courage to face the demons of your childhood as Colin has done. Behind all the macho stuff, there is in fact a pastoral care in the Army that particularly helps those with a difficult past and the sense of family is almost tribal. There will be occasions when you do something wrong and they will tear strips off you, but no one else is allowed to do it and that's quite a nice sort of feeling. That is why you can face such difficult situations with your close mates around you. The complete soldier knows when he needs to perform, when he needs to face danger, and he can do that and then come home to cut the grass. It's not easy, there are many that come back and complete suicide. That's what make the new chapters in Colin's life so interesting. Colin has made a fascinating start to his life already, but the adventure is just beginning!'

Andy McNab

PROLOGUE

The door slammed behind me and I heard it lock. Footsteps got gradually quieter and quieter and I tried to get up off the floor. I could feel the warm blood run down the side of my temple, and I couldn't see out my right eye, it was completely swollen shut. My ribs had a dull ache behind them from the kicks that had rained into them. I had eventually passed out and all the places that had been hit while I was unconscious slowly started reminding me. There was a small window in the room in the far corner and I went to see outside, or see if I could make my escape. The part of the window that opened was too small though. I weighed up my options, I could just wait it out and see if any help ever arrived, or I could try and just use force and bolt my way out the next time the door was unlocked. My meals were brought in on trays and there was a small window of opportunity. I would need to be fast and use everything I had. Even then, where would I go? But then … Who Dares Wins! I heard footsteps approaching and positioned myself near the door, but crouched over and looking slightly away from the door. Everything screamed in pain as I tensed my muscles, but I knew this would be about split seconds and surprise. Footsteps getting ever louder just like the thudding in my chest. The key in the lock, the click and then the creak of the door. I took a breath, tensed and then sprang at the shadow in the doorway…

When I showed my stepfather the initial draft of this book and he read this part he stopped, took a deep breath and looked skywards.

There was a long pause and he looked around the side of his chair for a handkerchief. Recognising the incident and his part in it, he looked at me with eyes full of tears and said, 'I'm sorry son'. I gave a sympathetic smile back 'Don't worry,' I said, 'it was just the start.' It had happened in 1988 and it wouldn't be the last time, or even the worst time I was stripped, beaten and left locked in a room. Life is like that sometimes. A journey with ups and downs – and sometimes the downs are as important, if not more so, in our lives. Our journey. As pilgrims.

CATALYSTS

*'For not an orphan in the wide world can be so deserted
as the child who is an outcast from a
living parent's love.'*
Charles Dickens, *Dombey and Son* (1848)

It seems strange, but look back at any time in your life, whether it's a holiday or some period at school, college or even work, and you always remember happy times, sunny days and cheery moments with friends. It always seems more difficult to remember those darker, sadder times, as if they're locked away in some shadowy recess, a labyrinth of emotions you maintain.

My childhood was nobody's idea of happy, and I couldn't grow up quickly enough, aching for the freedom to enjoy choices others take for granted. Yet what kind of future might rescue me, I had no idea. In the dark at home, as a youngster, I couldn't care less how it might all pan out. I can remember smiling, so I must have done it at times. I remember the grass under my feet, the smell of seasons as they raced by, short, cold, sunny days spent in the woods collecting berries or building dens. The rest I can barely recall, or just don't want to.

The unpalatable memories, when they do resurface, come in flickers like the fuzzy picture on an old-fashioned TV set in stormy weather, or the 'did that actually happen?' snippets that drift back to you after a heavy session on the ale the night before. The moments, thankfully, pass by as quickly as they start.

I was born in Edinburgh on Valentine's Day 1974, but whatever family life there might have been was short-lived. It ended when my father decided to leave while I was still very young. He had been working at a shipyard, according to Mum, and that's all I ever really knew about him.

As my toddling days came to an end, Mum would now be raising me alone. It was a situation I never really understood. I just knew that it was different to everyone else's life. I remember being dropped off at my gran's for a year while my mother disappeared off to Europe skiing, and at one point my gran wanted to raise me, but my grandfather advised her otherwise. We moved to Livingston when I was 2 or 3 and the first address I remember was 27 Larchbank, this would become apparent much later in life, and I went to nursery and my first year in primary school.

Not long after Dad left, we moved to the small village where I would attend school, a place that, to me, resembled a scene from the film *Cocoon*, where the ageing residents of a care home are mysteriously rejuvenated by a hidden alien influence. Woolfords must have been a wonderfully pleasant place for all the retired elderly people who resided there, with its single row of cottages, but it was so small that I could throw a stone from one end to the other, so for me it was an isolated island, and a million miles from civilisation.

With no social life to speak of outside of school, I lived from morning to night in my uniform. I had no need to wear any other clothes, as there was nowhere to go, nothing to do and no one to impress. With limitations placed on throwing stones along the length of the cottages, I made do with walks in the nearby woodland, roaming for hours with my best friend Romulus, an Irish setter. He was my only friend, and I loved every second I spent with my four-legged ally.

Things were about to change though, and looking back, I see that the next few years would have a profound effect on my life and provide the catalyst that would eventually change me more and push me further than I ever imagined or thought possible.

Summoned from my room one day after school, I was introduced to the man who would eventually become my stepfather. Benny was a broad man, thick-set across the shoulders, and with shovels for hands. He was one of those guys – a special investigator with the Social Services department – who take photographs from the back of a van of people scamming the dole. He came from a big Catholic family in Whitburn, which probably stopped him getting the living shit kicked out of him.

My mother was not religious at all, and would probably count as an atheist, although there was something Catholic about her fondness for discipline. There were rules in our house, chores to be done, and like most kids I was never allowed to leave the table until my dinner had been eaten, even though the mountain of potato could seem like Everest at times.

Why always potato, and why such volumes of it? When Mum wasn't watching I would flick spoonfuls in Rom's direction. He was grateful at first for the free carbs, but in the end even he grew tired of it and would sit there with a stupid stare and mash smeared all over his snout.

I had to get creative, and unluckily for Romulus his basket was the closest thing in reach that was out of sight of adults, so with methodical stealth I packed handfuls of mash around the palisade of wicker – so much that it eventually turned mouldy and offered a haven for flies. It wasn't my brightest idea, but Romulus didn't mind what I got up to.

My daily chores included washing the dishes, putting out the garbage, bringing the coal in, washing the car, lighting the fire and cleaning the floors. Then there was the usual polishing of shoes, and homework to do for next day. Walking Romulus was the only thing that didn't feel like a chore.

I was allowed to read a book in bed until 8.00 pm sharp, and my mother, in her prison-warden role, would always stop by at lights out. I felt a bit like a prisoner, even without the experience of how that would be. Failure to comply with any task might be met with physical punishment, and it was always my role – my responsibility, even – to fetch the instrument of torture, the wooden spoon. I hated the whole routine and thinking back I realise how humiliating and degrading it was to make me collect and hand over the instrument she meant to beat me with.

The resultant bruising would stretch from the small of my back to the tops of my thighs, leaving this strange, faded tartan look over my flesh. Sometimes she would slap me continuously in the face, all the time looking at me with such contempt. I was never quite sure why my mother hated me so much. I wasn't the one who had left; I was the one who paid the price.

I couldn't even put it down to unfinished chores – it was just the way things were. Maybe I wasn't achieving enough academically, maybe that crap thirty minutes' reading in my bed at night wasn't helping, or maybe it was simply that I was a boy. Deep down, that's how it felt.

Growing older, trying to progress through the years at school, I became aware of how other boys lived, and how school played such a minor part in their day. The real day for them began after school, when they would put their jeans on and meet up with their mates to play football or computer games, or even stay over at each other's houses. I yearned for this other semi-freedom and grew less interested in school.

I had no friends to speak of, and it was hard to make them when I was so reserved, lived too far from anyone else, and the only people that my permanent school uniform attracted were the bullies.

My mother's anger continued to grow, along with my lack of enthusiasm and effort at school. She warned me regularly of the perils of a poor education and told me in no uncertain terms that anything less than university would not be accepted in the family. My graduation picture must take pride of place next to the rest of the children at my gran's house.

The thing is, I always knew that I would have a picture, but I also knew that it would come from a very different graduation, one of my own choosing, and university couldn't have been further from my mind.

As the months passed, I grew more and more rebellious and loathed the thought of spending any more years in a classroom than absolutely necessary.

I saw myself as an actor. Joining a couple of small drama classes to avoid home, I embraced the freedom and began to relish the limelight, always taking centre stage in the school plays. Here I was a different person and became the character, any character, that I wanted to be, only too pleased to swap lifestyles. In real life I was miserable. On stage I was someone else – I was normal for an hour or so.

Moving schools meant that the acting stopped, but as sure as the days were long, the beatings increased, and with no end in sight I prayed to no one in particular that my mother would tire herself out with the wooden spoon, though more often it would snap before that happened.

It was usually only a matter of time before Benny, my stepdad, joined in. At first it was just lashings from his belt, but occasionally, when his rage got the better of him, he would fly at me with his fists and knock me to the ground.

One day my mum asked me to check that the front door was shut, and I headed towards the door. I was always on guard for my safety, and yet this time, out of nowhere, I felt an explosion of pain in my face. A fist sent me flying backwards over a chair in the living room, and the next thing I knew, Benny was standing over me looking menacing. Apparently, I hadn't been quick enough to shut the door and given my mother a 'look'. My eye swelled up like a balloon and within minutes I couldn't see out of it.

Looking at myself in the mirror in my room, I tried to muffle my sobs. I was in shock. 'Look at me', I thought. 'I'm a fucking wreck.' I was just a boy, surely this couldn't be right. Or did it happen to everyone at home?

'How do they hide it so well?' I thought. I wanted this, in some twisted way, to be normal, if only so that I could compare bruises and stories of beatings with other boys.

With no let-up in the chores, I was still expected to do, I scrambled down the stairs to go outside and empty the rubbish. Skulking along, I tried to hide from the outside world, but the next-door neighbour caught sight of me, and I heard my name. 'Colin, Colin', he shouted. 'Are you OK, wee man?' I ignored it, hoping that my eye wasn't seen.

Scurrying back into the house, I zipped quickly into my bedroom and sat gazing out of the window, hugging Romulus. I always felt that he knew I was in pain, because I knew how I felt about him, and every touch, paw or lick from him was a sign that there was still love to be had; that there was always hope of a better life.

Later that evening I was woken from my bed by my mum, who told me to get dressed, as there were some men who wanted to see me. Gingerly making my way from my room, I could see through the doorway two figures in the living room. I peered in and Mum said, 'There he is. Colin, these two men want a wee chat, so don't be talking any nonsense now, OK?'

There were two middle-aged men, both standing and staring straight at my face. The larger of the two spoke with an almost warm, understanding smile. 'What happened, Son?'

Petrified, I knew I couldn't tell them what had happened for fear I'd get more of the same when they left, so I just played dumb in the hope that someone else in the room would speak up.

It didn't take long. Mum could see my fear and explained that I had misbehaved, and my stepdad had simply caught me harder than he'd meant to, almost insinuating that I had somehow jumped onto Benny's punch.

The men told me that I must go with them to see a doctor for examination. More humiliation ensued as I stripped naked for the doctor to take pictures of my scrawny, bruised body from all sides. Returning me home, they explained that I would have visits from time to time and might have to go into a system called the 'Children's Panel' every few months or so.

It turned out that the neighbour I had tried to dodge had called the RSSPCC (Royal Scottish Society for the Prevention of Cruelty to Children) after noticing one too many bruises, and the NSPCC were also involved. In some ways I was glad he spoke out, but then again, the beatings never stopped, so I wasn't too sure what good it had done. Maybe it would provide police evidence should I be hit once too often!

The situation didn't improve at all, even when I was visited at home by social workers. I recall seeing how weak they were, and how they didn't fight for me. They allowed things to continue and were banished from the house by my mother.

Instead, my visits started to take place at school, during class hours, so now I had another humiliation to face: my beatings became the talk of the school. People were watching me so much that after one PT session I was in the shower when suddenly there was a mass exodus. Everyone just walked out of the shower block and left me there alone. Mr Boyd, our gym instructor, appeared and asked me to get dressed and report to his office. When I walked in he invited me to sit down, and he asked how things were at home.

Steely-eyed, I said: 'Everything is great, sir.' But he sat there silently and looked straight into my eyes, as if he could see everything. Bottom lip trembling, I tried to hold myself together, until he asked me to show him my back and legs and I saw the shock on his face and began to cry.

I realised then that my excuses of 'this must be normal' were utter shite. My head was in a mess, my feelings too. My shitty life, once hidden from everyone, was now common knowledge, and not to my advantage. A year or so would have to pass before a new abused kid took the spotlight from me. In the meantime, I was dumb enough to think that the worst was over. I was known as a damaged kid, and that should have been the end of it.

But then my mother became friendly with a younger man. His name was Tim, and by some twisted, fucked-up turn of fate he became my babysitter. I was getting on for 12 years old when he came onto the scene, and he was someone who I rarely spoke to or even thought about. I was usually in bed by the time he got to the house, which cut our interaction fairly short, the way I liked it.

What happened over the coming weeks, however, made me wish for a beating more than anything, and I would've been grateful for Benny to punch the shite out of me all night long instead. Benny was a drunk, and in some ways, I can see that he wasn't an evil soul – he probably just beat me the way his own father used to beat him. I know that many men beat their sons in the hope that they don't grow up to be weak, but I think that's not how it goes, and that too many beatings from a father will weaken any man.

Benny may have hit me harder, but it was Mum who put venom and hatred into what she did. She seemed to seek excuses for the next time, while Benny always seemed to resent having to do it.

The moon was up on this one particular night – not full, but enough to raise the level of light in my room – when I stirred and woke up, and realised I was desperate for a pee. I would have to pass Tim on my way to the bathroom, so I peered out of my bedroom door and asked if I could go to the toilet.

Easy enough. He said, 'Yes', so I climbed the stairs, did my stuff, and opened the bathroom door to leave only to find Tim standing there.

'All right?' I asked, and wondered what Tim was doing.

'Your ma says that I should teach you about things', he said. I knew something wasn't right, and then I found out why when he made me kneel beside him.

As the man I am today, it strikes me that Tim, my so-called babysitter, has had a lucky escape. In the depths of my mind, I will never tire of hurting Tim and his like.

The Children's Panel went on all through school and interfered with what little concentration I had left. I began to adjust my personality to suit, and made myself the extrovert I had dreamed of, like a character in a film. Playing the class clown, mimicking teachers, making wisecracks, I immersed myself in the wrong crowd in an effort to boost my popularity and self-esteem. I ended up on something called a Compulsory Supervision Order, where social workers had to see me and Children's Panel saw me in front of three strangers every six months.

As luck would have it, though, all was not lost. I was given a job down at the local farm over the weekends – the time when Tim would otherwise do most of his babysitting.

I was really grateful for the work. It instilled responsibility in me to run my different errands around the yard. Just to sweep and shovel was a dream, and before I knew it, I was driving the quad bike and tractor, ploughing fields and herding sheep during the summer when they needed shearing. My favourite task was catching them from the field and dragging them to the farmers in the shed.

The rest of the workers would watch and cheer me on as I went sprinting after the sheep to bring them in for clipping. There I was, in my first real relationship with men that didn't involve any humiliation.

Among so many other memories, this was the childhood I wanted to remember. Paid a pound a day, I opened my own Post Office account, and by saving every penny from birthdays or Christmas, I soon had enough to buy my own games console.

The Atari was launched, and I could afford to buy one. This was the life I craved: hard work – no problem; *Pac-Man*, *Asteroids*, *Space Invaders* – no problem either. My mind was free to dream, to make room for hopes of a better life. Little would I know that twenty years later I would be helping create some of the best video games the world has ever seen.

Events began to unfold that would change my life. Romulus died. In the course of four years my mum gave birth to my little brother and two sisters. There might be a massive age gap between us, but now I was carrying the 'big brother' tag. My new siblings were my life, and I would ensure at all costs that they knew what the love of a big brother meant.

Then an unscheduled appearance before the Children's Panel had me worried I'd be carted off to the local foster home. Mum woke me the night before and said that I had to mind what I said, because if I went to a children's home, I might never see my little brother or sisters again. I was devastated, flooded with anguish. The next day I held back when talking to the panel and was relieved when I was allowed to stay at home.

Life continued and, whatever my own troubles, I was happy to watch my siblings like a hawk. I was at the age, also, when Tim no longer needed to babysit. I had grown an inner resilience to physical violence and being able to suffer. I was able to control my emotions when things got bad and this resilience was about to become my superpower. The thing that would help me throughout my life and help when pain, rejection, failure and physical punishment all came calling. I realise now, how much a 'childhood' is important and sets you on a trajectory in life. How it shapes you for the future and how those experiences, positive or negative, shape you into what you become later in life. Those experiences have not been lost on me; I remember them to this day and they guide me through the Children's Panel as a chair on the other side of the table to this very day.

My school grades were not that impressive, so my mother was convinced that there would be no university place for me. I have since learned that being happy at home gives you a better chance of being successful at school. Many years later, I would end up revisiting school and university and would gain a First-Class MA Honours degree, as well as Best Dissertation, Best in History and Best Student; up to that point, I was the only student to have won all three academic awards and, as far as I know, it hasn't been done since then either. I was the same person with the same brain, just in a better place. My mother looked for other ways to see the back of me, and when she found out that my aunt's husband was in the British Army, he was frogmarched to the house to set eyes on me. That meant that he looked me over from head to toe and back, shot a disapproving glare, and sneered, 'He may make sergeant.'

According to my mum, I was to be out of the house by my sixteenth birthday, so the very next day I was dragged down to the local recruiting office and met by a burly man with a handlebar moustache who stood upright and shook my hand firmly before planning out the next twenty-two years of my life. It was music to my mother's ears. I didn't have a say.

Tests back then were fairly straightforward, and I passed with ease. With that, the recruiting sergeant said I could go wherever I wanted, so I pointed to one of the posters on the wall, impressed by the well-tanned man fixing what looked like a satellite dish in some exotic climate. 'Could I join his unit?' I asked. 'Yes', was his answer, 'this is a telecommunication systems analyst operator, but you'll be on a year's waiting list.' My mother shook her head and said I was to be out the house by the time I was 16.

The sergeant shook his own head in exasperation at my mum's insistence, like he had heard this before. 'An infantry intake starts in three weeks', he said, and with that my fate was sealed.

Whenever you find yourself in despair and in a rut. Rejection, failure and people looking at you like your worthless, remember: it's just the present and everyday won't be like this. Just put one foot in front of the other.

DEPOT

It was 1989 and the start of my new life was playing out to an eclectic musical soundtrack. Aboard a smoke-filled minibus travelling to the army's junior leaders' depot on the outskirts of Newcastle, Tears for Fears' Beatles' pastiche *Sowing the Seeds of Love* drifted from the trashy radio, barely audible above the noise of the engine and the chatter of conversation. The psychedelic pop was swiftly followed by Technotronic's *Pump up the Jam*, but the quick switch to hip house made little impression on minds that were clearly elsewhere.

Looking around at the rest of our group, I could see that the young lads seemed noticeably more eager than I was to reach our destination, and keener still to pump the soldier driving us for whatever information he might have about where we were going. He offered none, and kept resolutely silent, opening his mouth only to accommodate the three cigarettes he smoked on the journey.

Drawing close to what looked like a main gate, the taciturn driver brought the minibus to a steady halt at what seemed little more than a bus stop minus any shelter, before turning his head just enough to give us all a hostile look via his rear-view mirror. 'Right, grab your shit and get the fuck off my bus', he snarled.

Smiles about me turned to frowns, and you could see and feel that the penny had just dropped for the eager beavers. Shoulders started to droop, and the sudden realisation that this was not the cosy summer camp they'd dreamed of made for a tense sixty seconds. I thought for a split second about coming back with a funny to fill the now awkward silence. Wisely, however, the 'How would you like us to get the fuck off your bus?' quip stayed safe in the back of my mind.

Surveying the soulless, square-edged buildings with their complete lack of colour, I felt like I'd come to a prison camp. Groups of people were walking around in unnaturally straight lines and punishments were being dealt out on every corner.

My peripheral vision was interrupted by a group of five young men carrying what appeared to be fitted wardrobes. If that was not unusual enough, these wardrobes were full of neatly folded military attire. Next came their beds, and then a desk. They were making their way to a concrete square where they were laying out make-believe living quarters, placing their furniture as if fitting it into a virtual bedroom. I recall thinking how stupid it was and wondering why on earth they were doing it.

Without warning, a mattress was hurled from a window, followed by a wardrobe. 'What the fuck is happening here?' I said quietly to another lad. 'That will be us soon', he replied, ominously. I wanted to go home. Suddenly it seemed a nicer place. 'Has Mum actually sent me to a nuthouse for messing up at school?' I thought, with a nervous inner laugh.

There was no time to adjust before a tall man appeared in an immaculate army uniform and yelled at us to hurry off the bus and stand in one straight line, side by side.

Answering to our names, we were each assigned to different-numbered buildings. I was being sent to a place called Minden Platoon, so I grabbed my belongings and set off with a smaller group of lads with the same destination.

As we walked through the heavy double doors of one of the soulless buildings, I noticed the same fireproof windows that we'd had at school, the ones with wire mesh running through the glass. But this place was a far cry from school.

Traipsing down a long corridor, I looked at the pictures that covered the walls. Guns and maps; soldiers in camouflage, in different positions, some lying down and some standing or kneeling.

I stared at the shiny floor. It was immaculate, spotless. 'Mum would like this', I grinned to myself as I followed the other lads through a door into our quarters.

There were six of us to a room. Each of us sized up a small space holding just a bed and locker, and I picked a corner plot before dropping the two holdalls that contained my entire life heavily onto the floor.

Fast forward two months and my bed was in a state of permanent perfection, most of us opting to sleep on the floor and allow our crisply ironed sheets, neat hospital corners and ruler-measured blocks of spare bed sheets and blankets to remain totally undisturbed. Our lockers were now havens of symmetry and straight lines, boasting razor-sharp creases and corners, not so different to my first impression of this camp where dullness ruled.

For most of my early training my locker stayed far from the best. I was a poor barracks soldier, and I am the first to admit that this would dog me throughout all the years I served. I was a 'soldier' better placed out on the ground, covered in mud and doing 'in-the-field' soldiering.

'Where is the toughest place you've soldiered, Col?' is among the mass of questions I've come in for over the years from blokes in the pub about my different deployments or the locations I've served in, and it is one of the easiest to answer – straight off, without a doubt – 'In barracks!'

I found barrack soldiering hugely claustrophobic, but then, while still pushing 16, I was one of the least-developed lads in my intake of boys up to 18 years old, so it's fair to say that I found almost everything in training a shitty routine and a tough experience. Many of the other volunteers revelled in the constant hurry or striving for perfection, but I was far from a volunteer, and although I was used to strict discipline, it wasn't the life that I'd chosen, nothing I'd wanted.

Our instructors homed straight in on my dislike of being there and kept on asking if I wanted to quit and go home. Maybe if I'd been given the choice after that quick unloading from the bus on that first day, I might have taken it, but for once I found a sense of belonging – I belonged to this platoon. Something was changing inside me, and for the first time I began to make proper friends, people that I could rely on, and who relied on me. Having said that, the alternative was far worse. I would never have wanted to go back home and knew that my life there was far worse.

As I began to enjoy the sense of achievement I felt when I collapsed, exhausted, at the end of each day, I was reminded of my happy days spent at the farm. I didn't want to fail. I can't stand the saying, but it rang true for me back then that 'failure was never an option'. Whether it was to show something to my mother, or for the sake of my brother and sisters, or for myself, I had begun to understand a bit about pride and what it meant, and I decided to knuckle down and give this new career a fair shot.

I never once spoke to my mother, and if I'd hated her way back before she packed me off into the army, then it had grown into something else by now. I received letters from her as the year drew to a close, but it didn't cross my mind to reply. My grandmother was a different story, though. I cherished her letters and loved her dearly. She genuinely cared about me and hadn't the slightest idea about the life I had grown to despise with her daughter.

Learning fast, it was soon clear to me that I wasn't the only one in the army from a broken or dysfunctional home. It was commonplace there. Yet I do have some fond memories of my time in training, though I also remember how much I looked forward to it when we were all given a week's leave just three months into it.

We were all paid just £5 every week, so that the remainder could be placed in the bank for when we went on leave, but my excitement was dashed when, after twelve weeks of hard work, the older recruits walked out with £300 while I received a mere £65. I was told it was because of my age. It didn't seem fair to work as hard as everyone else but get paid less, and I was annoyed to have so little.

All the same, it didn't deter me from my main goal for the week's leave, which was to try to track down my real father. With my rail warrant ready, I headed north to Glasgow intending to search around the Oban area, based on the only snippets of information I had managed to glean about my dad.

I spent the first two nights in a bed and breakfast but had found no information so pressed on. Then, as the third night began to draw in with the same blank achieved, a glimmer of hope came with the news that there might be a family matching my surname in the area. I eventually tracked them down, but couldn't get to see them, sadly spending my last two days working on a nearby farm to earn the remainder of my keep before hitching back to Glasgow train station. My mother had always given me her surname, Pithie, but my actual surname was my father's from my birth certificate, which was Maclachlan, so armed with this I ventured around my father's family area in Oban and Loch Fyne to try and trace my family and a better existence.

Arriving back at the depot, I felt tired and completely demoralised, especially with gleeful fellow recruits swapping tales of fun and debauchery from their own week's leave. I was to find out many years later, in a bitter letter from my mother, that my father had died in Oban around the same week that I was looking for him there, that was a hard pill to swallow.

So near and yet so far. I have still failed to find many links with that side of my family, and there is a whole missing part of my personal jigsaw. It's one of the many questions I haven't resolved. Somewhere out there are parts of my family who have no idea who I am, and the life I have led. But I haven't lost hope. Maybe one outcome of writing this book is that I will find them, or they'll have a chance to find me.

After another month back in the cycle of training, we were allowed, and indeed encouraged, to attend a disco held on camp every Friday night. Local girls were invited, so as to give it an air of normality, though the backdrop of lurking instructors made that impossible as they ran watchful eyes over their charges.

Cramming ourselves into dark corners in a flurry of fumbling hands and heavy breathing, and all without the benefit of alcohol, the scene could hardly have been further from normal, but I did meet a girl who must go down officially as my first girlfriend. We would meet every Friday at the disco, where we would hide in the shadows and kiss like a pair of mating goldfish.

Halfway through our training we were given a long weekend, and she asked if I wanted to stay with her, as her parents were away. I lustfully agreed and was young and stupid enough to go around telling my colleagues that I was staying with my 17-year-old girlfriend who had her own car.

Sure enough, Friday came, and there she was in her little Mini Metro, waiting outside the gates to pick me up. I looked a total mess, as we had just completed our first mini exercise, where we'd had to build a shelter and stay up all night, surviving on our rations and imagining we were Rambo.

I was exhausted, dishevelled and excited all at once, and then, as she drove us away, she broke the worst of all news for a teenage boy bursting at the seams with testosterone. Her parents were not going away just yet, she told me. They just wanted to meet me before they headed to their caravan for the weekend.

When I arrived at the house, I timidly walked into the living room to be met by both parents, a smelly dog and a huge old-fashioned three-bar electric fire that was so hot I was sure it was melting the paisley-patterned wallpaper. I sat down in front of it, and straight away felt desperately tired as the fatigue from the previous night's exercise set in. All the same, I had to do my best to appear interested as her father told me about his father being in the army during the war and … yada yada yada…

I could feel my heavy eyelids growing heavier, and I fought to raise my head in the vain attempt to maintain eye contact with her father, to listen to the torrent of his words, but it was just too hot in the room and my eyes felt sore and tired, as if they were full of smoke, and I drifted off to sleep…

I woke up with a start and realised that my girlfriend had been elbowing me in the ribs, so I looked at her parents and saw, in a burst of alarm, that they weren't even talking any more. They were just sitting and staring with horrified expressions on their faces.

I looked back at my girlfriend, who was motioning towards the door and raising her eyebrows as if to signal me up the stairs. So, I went to get up off the couch, and that triggered the most heart-stopping feeling I had ever had. I was wearing tight tracksuit bottoms called Ronhills, and as I stood up I could feel I had the most conspicuous erection possible!

I could feel my face burning red, flushing as hot as the fire, and all I could do was blurt out a babble of apologies as, with my knees only just keeping me upright, I staggered through the door and upstairs to the safety of the bathroom. I locked the door and proceeded to pour cold water on my groin. From below came the sound of my girlfriend's parents shouting at her, and then a door slammed shut and there was silence.

She came up and knocked on the door, and I answered, dreading the flood of abuse that was bound to follow, but instead she erupted into fits of uncontrollable laughter as she explained to me how I had fallen asleep while groaning and gyrating away in the chair, getting louder and louder until she had no choice but to halt my erotic fever!

The exertions of the training exercise might have left me exhausted, but whatever overnight manoeuvres I had hoped to get up to with my girlfriend were not now going to reach the intended conclusion. It didn't surprise me to learn that her parents had refused to have me stay for the weekend.

Anyone showing potential was rewarded with rank at the junior depot, and even though this was only a junior rank, and had no effect on pay or career, it meant less work and more responsibility for those blessed with the stripes on their arms (no different to real rank, I guess!).

I hadn't received any stripes throughout all of my training and couldn't claim much of a hope when it came to the award for best combat infantryman at the end of the year. We all had a heap of tasks to perform – some mental, some physical, and even some drill. I found myself coasting through, until eventually there were only two of us left. Unfortunately, for me, it was the 18-year-old junior colour sergeant who had made it through with me and he was hot favourite to win the award.

We were given a shooting competition on the range as a decider, and we both hit twenty out of twenty, so there was still no separating us. Next we were told to go down a live range, with targets popping up at random positions to be scored on. As we set off, I chose to peel left into a small stream and waded through, taking up occasional fire positions to shoot at the odd target, while my opposite number had decided to use the high ground and was patrolling along the ridgeline, again stopping now and then to fire.

We came to the end of the range, the hits were counted, and to my disbelief we both had twenty out of twenty again! The instructors huddled together and there was a quick round of whispering before they emerged and announced that my opposite number should win due to the better choice of ground.

I couldn't believe it and tried hard to argue my case, but it cut no ice. There I was, 16 years old and a novice, trying to argue my case against people much older and with vast experience. This was a trait I would take with me for the rest of my career.

I passed out on 15 December 1990 and was officially a soldier, but I was only 16, and – in what felt like further punishment – not allowed to join my chosen regiment (1st Battalion the Royal Scots) because I was too young to go to Germany.

Instead, I had to stay on the base at the depot until I reached 17. My mother and grandmother had come to see me pass out, but I never spoke to my mother, I briefly thanked my gran and left straight away with a friend and spent that leave in Dundee. Now I was a master of my own destiny. I would hardly ever see my mother again.

Whenever you're in a place where you feel imposter syndrome, or you don't seem to fit in. Remember that quite often it's a reflection of others' perception and not your ability or qualities. I've had it my whole life and I've accepted it will generally always be there. I had it for people judging me on my military acumen and I joined the SAS, I had it for education and I ended up top of the First-Class Honours list. Control the controllable.

OPERATION GRANBY

I was too young to be sent to Germany but the First Gulf War of 1990 was kicking off so I was sent down to Cambridge to do my Op Granby training with a different Scottish infantry unit called the Royal Highland Fusiliers. From my time in the depot I knew of a couple of the lads that had gone there, and this Glasgow-based unit had a real reputation for playing hard and fighting hard. There was a lot of drinking and fighting, and around a year earlier the unit had returned from providing support at the Lockerbie air disaster where the Pan-Am flight was blown up killing 270 people, including 11 people on the ground. I had to grow up quick and did my pre-deployment training for the Gulf there.

We were lined up and out of the dozen or so of us there, half were sent to Iraq and the other were sent to report to The Royal Scots in Werl, where they were based as an armoured mechanised battalion in Warrior armoured personnel carriers or APCs. I was to be part of the rear party but would be deployed in three months' time when I was old enough. Having left the Royal Highland Fusiliers as they departed for the Gulf, I remember being told about a time a year or so later, after they had returned to the UK, where a couple of lads been done in by the local – and quite large – Gypsy community in Cambridge. The next day the entire unit formed up and advanced on the Gypsy camp site and obliterated it, chasing the Gypsy community out of Cambridge. They were a mad bunch indeed and that was my induction into the real man's army! Little would I know that not far away a certain Andy McNab would be about to write a chapter in SAS history that I would be following...

'If I have seen further,
it is by standing on the shoulders of giants.'

Isaac Newton

THE ROYAL REGIMENT

Time passed by, and before I knew it my sorry young carcass had made its way to Werl, in Germany, where I finally got to join my unit. As the 4-tonner pulled into the barracks I was amazed to see two heads that appeared over the top of the tailgate of the vehicle, meaning these guys were at least 6 feet, 4 inches. John Lothian and John Gaylor were members of the battalion's RP, or Regimental Police, staff and were absolutely massive. I thought, *wow what are they feeding these guys here?* as they lifted me practically single-handedly out the vehicle onto the parade square. We were given our respective companies, I was destined for A Company and headed over.

An armoured battalion of fighting-age men was a world away from the cosy surroundings I had just left, and with no bunting or welcome party I had to be quick to pick up the nuts and bolts of working around grizzled, battle-hungry men before I was allowed anywhere near the mechanics of kit or equipment.

After a week or so I was given a set of green coveralls and taken down to an old hangar housing the battalion vehicles. I heard a well-rehearsed descriptive overview of the Warrior. 'Twenty-five tons of aluminium; an armoured personnel carrier or APC; it was designed to keep up with the Challenger 2 tank, moving troops around the battlefield; it offers relative cover from small arms; it can be fitted with…' the detail seemed endless, and not paying as much attention as I should have to this cumbersome piece of kit would have a huge impact on my life further down the track.

I was not too sure what I was expecting when I arrived in Germany, but it soon became clear that I was back at the bottom of the food chain, an automatic candidate for any and all shit jobs. Trying to gauge who I could trust with my thoughts about the tough new environment I had landed in, I found out that it wasn't uncommon in the battalion to be a private soldier still in your early thirties.

Surely, I thought, I wouldn't be doing these shit jobs for the next fifteen years? Looking back later, I realised that shit jobs always need to be done, regardless of rank or years served, and you learned to enjoy these tasks because they were usually the ones where you were left alone.

Those senior jocks in their thirties ran the platoons from the inside like sergeant majors, with no need for stripes on their arms. They hated new recruits and took a personal interest in ensuring our suffering and seeing to it that we were kept busy. The first sign of salvation for me came from a chirpy, fresh-faced lad called Axel, who had been in the intake before me and was full of useful advice and top tips for easing the way.

Arriving from depot into a world of hardened soldiers was daunting enough, but this new world was supercharged with extra testosterone as the battalion prepared for battle. The completion of my junior leaders' training and the transfer to unit, had taken place against a backdrop of international tension building up to the First Gulf War.

The Iraqi dictator Saddam Hussein had sent his troops into neighbouring Kuwait in August 1990, and the Americans had assembled the largest military coalition since the Second World War in response, so the chances of conflict seemed more and more inevitable, and the battalion carried out endless days of pre-deployment training – training that I wouldn't get the chance to put to use.

Security Council Resolution 678 of 29 November 1990, which gave Iraq a six-week deadline to get out of Kuwait, was the starting gun for the lead elements of the battalion to head for the Gulf as part of Operation Granby, and it wasn't long before the main battalion was deployed, but once again my age prevented me from taking part, so the only action I was resigned to seeing was sweeping out the hangars back at base. Every man 17½ was sent to the Gulf, but for me, just two months shy, rear party beckoned. I was left behind to guard our main base in Werl until one of two things happened: either I was old enough to deploy or the war had ended.

It was tough watching everyone leave. They were excited about the prospect of getting blooded, and it was hard not to immerse myself in their mixture of enthusiasm and trepidation. I had trained for this moment, and I wanted to have a go, naïve enough to long for real-life combat.

At least while the battalion was deployed, I discovered what a beautiful place Germany was, its countryside filled with expansive woodland in which I could get lost for hours, running around. I might not have been at war in the Gulf, but I was getting blooded in a different way. At the tender age of 17 I was discovering alcohol, betting and the red-light district. My eager eyes were popping out of my head. With no debt, and a decent wage going into the bank every month, I could spend my cash on anything I liked.

My needs were basic, like most men's, and I was growing up fast around older, more experienced soldiers. Learning about the qualities expected in the army, I came to see that respect for others was foremost among them – something I felt was lacking in my childhood. I loved to say 'please' and 'thank you' to civilians, regardless of their title. I may have been the politest young customer the red-light district had ever seen!

My rear-party holiday was short-lived as the battalion began to return in dribs and drabs. One battalion member had made the ultimate sacrifice, and this was the first of many coffins I would carry and funerals I would attend.

Once the initial sorrow of losing one of our own began to wane, our regiment was full of tales of valour and heroes. Medals were talked about before everyone was sent on leave to spend much-deserved time with their families.

No sooner was everyone back than it was time to clean and service everything, as we were to be posted back to Scotland. Our fate was to spend the next four years at Fort George, an old but well-preserved fort just outside Inverness, where the wind blew in relentlessly from the Moray Firth and battered the walls of this rickety old landmark.

Fort George had been erected as a base for government troops after the Jacobite rebellion in 1745, and the last battle fought on British soil, at Culloden in 1746, was only a few miles away. The area itself was saturated in history, and most of the places of interest within the fort were open to the general public.

Inverness was only 12 miles away, and we would often share a taxi into town at the weekend, or venture back home in one of the older guys' cars. I was settling into battalion life nicely and making solid friends along the way. I was moved to C Company, or Charlie Company, and quickly made friends.

I couldn't help but notice during the coming years that the Scottish regiments spent a fair amount of their time in Northern Ireland, and sure enough it was soon our turn, and for me the first of three six-month tours of South Armagh.

Bandit country, as we called it, loomed ominously – or the way I saw it, the chance had arrived to do some real soldiering; active patrolling, day and night; and OPs, or observation posts, for up to three weeks at a time, laying up overnight in bushes or hides.

I felt at home here, navigating off a map with live rounds in my magazines, facing a real and dangerous enemy. The IRA, or Irish Republican Army, and their activists knew those areas like the backs of their hands and could suss out nearly every vehicle using 'dickers' (lookouts) everywhere.

We stayed in small makeshift bases, planted in the middle of small towns, equipped with helipads and hard shelters with a watchtower at every corner, and we were sent out twice, maybe three times a day around our different areas of responsibility, now more commonly known as AO, or area of operations. It's a handy way to divide up ground to be covered to best use the manpower you have.

On the base I would take my turn on guard duty, remaining alert through the dark hours before changing shift with the other lads manning the watchtowers, or sangars as we called them. (The word comes from the North-West Frontier of India, back in the days of the British Raj.) During one of my sangar duties, one late afternoon, I was standing alone in the tower just 'monging' or allowing my mind and imagination to take me wherever I wanted to be. With a cursory check of my arcs of fire I spotted a tall man, his face blackened, wearing a combat jacket and heading into one of the nearby houses carrying a large bag.

The adrenalin rush nearly knocked me off my feet as I grabbed the intercom system before shouting loudly: 'STAND TO, STAND TO!' My panicked warbling continued and all I managed was: 'Terrorist wearing a balaclava has just gone … er, I mean walked into, ah, 27 such-and-such avenue, and he's carrying a bag!'

I was ordered to train my machine gun on the front door as the QRF, the Quick-Reaction Force, was deployed. My heart raced. This was my big moment. This was the terrorist attack that I was about to foil. The one I had thought about during six months of pre-deployment training.

What would the CO say to me? Maybe I wouldn't be a 30-year-old private soldier; maybe I was destined for corporaldom sooner than that!

My reverie was interrupted by the clatter of a helicopter flying low overhead to land less than 100 feet from the house I was anxiously aiming at. Around a dozen RUC, or Royal Ulster Constabulary men jumped out, running in a straight line to the front garden along with the small army patrol that had just gone out from our base. There was a slight pause as the group spoke briefly and then a loud crash as the front door went in.

I waited for what seemed like hours, imagining the dramatic manoeuvres that must be going on inside – 'Room clear! Room clear!' – as the soldiers and police swept the house of terrorists before discovering the huge arsenal of weaponry.

Suddenly, the place fell quiet, the silence interrupted only by the laughter of the soldiers leaving the house. I could see some of them shaking their heads, confused, and I could only wonder what had happened. The intercom kicked back into life again and, louder than normal, I heard a voice yell out, 'Maclachlan, report to the OC's office when you come off!'

I smirked naïvely, wishing the time away so I could face my OC and his admiration for a job very well done. Even if it was only a test, I had passed it with flying colours, and the battalion of war heroes would now see how alert and highly vigilant I was. Possible early promotion was looming.

My stag (guard duty) finally finished; I raced to the OC's office. He was behind his desk when I arrived, and he looked straight up at me and said, 'Ahh, Maclachlan, you've caused quite a stir.' Smiling with enthusiasm I responded, 'Just doing my job, sir', my chest close to bursting.

'Mm, well, it seems you thought you saw a man with a balaclava walking into a nearby address. It turns out that you spotted the only coloured man living in the entirety of South Armagh.'

'Holy shit!' I thought. My cheeks reddened, my shoulders dropped and I looked down at the floor for any escape. No promotion for this junior jock, just an onslaught of jokes and wisecracks from every corner about my observation skills. I was devastated, but the OC could see that and just told me to be more careful and 100 per cent sure next time. I nodded my head and slunk away. It was a lesson learned, and my wandering mind became a lot more focused from then on, as did my reporting skills.

The tour was a success, overall, right up until the final month when one of our battalion was shot and killed by a sniper just days before we were due to return. It was a shattering blow, not least because he was a very popular soldier who had a brother, also in the battalion. Lawrence Dickson was stationed at Forkhill with me in South Armagh and was in the team just in front of me as we patrolled the area. We heard the shot and I didn't quite see what happened but the sniper who had been operating in that area had made Lawrence his fourth victim. It was St Patrick's Day 1993. I didn't know at the time, but less than six years later I would join the sub unit that captured him. It angers and frustrates me that the Good Friday Agreement let terrorists go despite being convicted of murder, yet even today serviceman and women are dragged through the courts and imprisoned for serving their country and the wishes of the very politicians who later targeted them.

Still nursing what may seem like a ridiculous personal anti-climax, I put the post-Northern Ireland tour blues on hold, safe in the knowledge that at least I'd had the luck to make it home. By now I had a solid group of muckers to hang out with on leave. We were mostly from the same platoon, and as thick as thieves. Coming from areas in and around Edinburgh, we took advantage of the bustling city with its great shops, nightlife and constant waves of tourists who kept the high streets thriving. My only diversion from this direct route to the city's high spots was a swift visit to see my brother and sisters. I may have been running from a lot of things, but they weren't one of them. Selfish or not to have gone off on the run from my shitty circumstances – as if I'd had the ghost of a choice – I hoped they'd find a better deal in store. I don't mind admitting, I wasn't strong enough to have stuck around. I would have ended up in jail or worse.

Returning from leave, however, I had an extra spring in my step. For once life was tabbing along pretty smoothly … until I heard the words 'battalion boxing competition'. In my world this ought to have been a bit of fun – gloves on, a couple of rounds and then on the lash – but no chance. In good army-organised order, people were randomly paired and told to show no mercy, to attack until the opponent was unconscious or dead.

Not much of a boxer, I nevertheless had innate fitness on my side, a solid engine beneath a deceptive body, and being far better at avoiding punches than throwing them, I could at least stay the distance. From the carnage of pre-selection, my fitness earned me a place on the boxing team, but that was just the start.

Told to lose half a stone in two weeks, I looked in the mirror and thought, 'Where is that coming from?' I was 8 stone, soaking wet. My happy return from leave had come to a grinding halt of misery, and two weeks of eating little more than lettuce and apples turned me into something akin to a famine victim.

I shadow-boxed for an eternity in the sauna wearing a bin liner. A final punishing series of sit-ups and press-ups in the same unrelenting heat eventually ensured I made the weight, and I was carried, barely conscious, through to the weigh-in before being dumped on the scales.

Next day, the fun really started and I was straight into the qualifiers. A whirlwind of fights later, I had managed to win my way into the final against 'Bulldog' Walker, a thickset young officer.

Not only was I up against an officer, but ours was also the last fight of the evening, and my company was standing joint first with one of the other fighting companies. It was all down to my scrawny frame against 'Bulldog' Walker. I knew that he'd boxed as an officer in training at Sandhurst, and he looked a lot stronger than me, but I was slightly taller, if that counted for anything. I knew there was a lot of money being staked on the outcome of the bout, and my own sergeant major had firmly advised me to win!

The battalion was all in attendance and making a hell of a noise, but when the bell rang I heard none of it. Walker came out fists flying everywhere, and I did just enough to stay upright in the first few seconds, ducking and sliding around until, eventually, I managed to compose myself.

I knew that I couldn't win in a slugging match, so I used my jab to keep my distance and my fitness to keep moving. Then, just when I thought I'd made it safely through the first round, he caught me in the temple and I dropped to one knee.

My coach was screaming from our corner, complaining to the ref that I'd been elbowed and not punched, but he was ignored. Looking up at him, I could see him mouth some words – 'Get up at eight.' I remember just staring at him and asking, 'What time is it at the minute?' He just laughed and I stood back up and finished the round.

The next round went better. I'd learnt my lesson, and if there was one thing I was good at it was getting hit and getting back up. I started to impose myself on the 'Bulldog', and by the third round I felt comfortable and even went toe-to-toe for a while, but soon reverted back to smarter tactics.

As the seconds were counted down, I knew I had done enough to win. I was thrilled to get a standing ovation after the final bell, not just for winning but for being awarded best boxer of the competition, and to this day my name is still proudly etched on the trophy.

A few months later I found that I'd climbed up the food chain and was now being put forward for promotion. This was exciting: rank had its privileges, and I would receive a pay rise if I passed the six-week cadre (selection course). Not only that, but I'd be relieved of many of the mundane daily tasks that I'd got accustomed to. Promotion would see me now supervising the cleaning of the toilets, the picking up of litter around camp and the collection of stores when they were needed.

Determined to do well, I was physically fit, confident and good at speaking (or gobbing off) in front of an audience. Little did I know then, but many years later I would be making a career of motivational speaking. It will be no surprise to anyone how much of a leveller an infantry promotion course can be, and this would be my first taste of just how much fatigue and the pressure of leadership brings out the best and worst in people. As well as the hardships, though, there were many funny moments on my cadre, and some stay with me even now.

One particular morning we were all lined up for a room and locker inspection. Being a jack-the-lad, I'd been out the night before with my friend Frankie, and my locker was in its usual state – which meant not really ready for inspection. On the other hand, the soldier in the bed space next to mine was sheer perfection, his immaculate turnout making my own look even worse, if that was possible.

Smirking at his own cleverness, he then made the mistake of asking out loud what time he had to report sick at the medical centre – any excuse to get out of PT. A cunning plan entered my psyche. 'You're late, should've been there five minutes ago!' I said, half-jokingly. Away he went, darting straight out of the room, and the moment he moved I took a quick step sideways to stand proudly in front of his locker just before the instructors walked in.

The inspection started, and our instructor walked up to the space where I was standing, then looked at me, looked at my locker, and looked at me again before his attention shifted onto my friend's new junk-pile inheritance. 'What creature owns this?' he snarled. I reluctantly informed him, then watched as he ran down the corridor in the direction of the medical centre. My friend might not escape PT after all.

Every weekend we would go home, and every weekend someone else would play 'the numbers game'. This was basically hoping that, if everybody else had the same task or lesson to do, then the likelihood of you getting picked was slim, and you could save precious time on the planning and preparation by simply not doing whatever it was.

My own time came for Russian roulette, and I chose the weekend we were instructed to plan a basic set of orders. So, sure as shit, I was the one picked first thing Monday morning to give that set of orders to the entire class. 'Orders' meant plans that you had to think out in every detail. They contained every feature from dress and equipment to key timings and how you hoped to achieve your aim, and they could cover anything from an ambush to a simple reconnaissance patrol.

I looked to the floor in despair, my head crammed full of visions racked with inevitable failure, and then, without warning – a sign from the gods – I saw a full set of orders lying on the floor I was staring at. The soldier sitting next to me had left his neatly written plans there; it was like he knew my plight, or I'd just become the luckiest man on the planet.

I calmly bent down and picked them up before launching straight into 'my' orders, pausing only to pose occasional questions in a bid to read ahead in their provisions. I was narrowly beaten to the 'best student' award, but I was pleased, nevertheless, because I was soon promoted and on my way up the rank ladder. Well, one rung up it, at least.

'What lies behind us, and what lies before us,
are tiny matters
compared to what lies within us.'
Ralph Waldo Emerson

MY HOME IS MY CASTLE

With my course completed, our battalion went into immediate pre-deployment training, of a particularly rigorous kind, as we prepared in earnest for our next call of duty. But this would be no routine engagement. The Royal Scots were to guard Edinburgh Castle, and that meant confronting a dreaded enemy ... relentless hours of gruelling drill and inspections.

I hated drill with a passion. It bored me, marching up and down over and over again before being crucified for having a floating speck of cotton out of place, or a smear on a brass button, or shiny toecaps not of the gloss expected. But there was one lad who, I guess, hated drill even more than me.

Our company fielded quite an array of characters, some of them from a similar or worse background than my own, and considerably more volatile. Memories of my life come in waves, rolling in from the distance, but I remember this moment as if it were five minutes ago, and I still have to laugh at the thought of it.

Rewind the clock, if you will, to a time in the mid-1990s, to a parade ground in Edinburgh, and an inspection by our RSM, regimental sergeant major, the most senior soldier in the battalion.

The RSM made his way up the line of poker-straight soldiers, their buttons sparkling, toecaps burnished to within an inch of their lives, necks locked to attention. Suddenly he stopped at the soldier standing right next to me, and I wondered what he'd spotted. There'd be no reason to stop other than to find fault: you were never congratulated on a good turnout.

Staring hard at the soldier's feet, the RSM pointed to his victim's shoes, or 'brogues', then gestured towards his face with his pace stick, poking it deliberately too close for comfort, before announcing in a loud and angry tone, 'There's a piece of shite on the end of my pace stick!'

Silence fell on the entire square. This was the kind of moment you were glad someone else was having to take the RSM's wrath, except this soldier had no intention of taking it. 'Not at this end, sir', he told the most senior man in the battalion.

As a company of men heard it, so too could you hear the gasp of air sucked in by every man. A flurry of fists and shouts of outrage followed as my comrade decided to take things a stage further. In for a penny, in for a pound. He beat the RSM with his own pace stick before he could be dragged off to jail by the fast-arriving Regimental Police, who for obvious reasons had to be some of the toughest men in battalion.

The castle was a great place to be, especially in the summer. We would wear our smart uniforms, or 'number ones', and spend most of the time peacocking around the grounds, occasionally posing for photographs or accepting phone numbers and addresses from admiring female tourists who were passing.

As a lance corporal, I would normally stand at the entrance of the castle in between two private soldiers – jocks, as we call them. They stood in two sentry boxes, occasionally marching to and fro before throwing in some smart-looking rifle drill, much to the delight of our foreign visitors.

At night time we would stay at the castle itself as part of our guarding duties. High times were had, either dressing up in one of the waxworks' uniforms to frighten passers-by, or making up far-fetched stories for the tourists who visited late at night.

It kept us from getting bored, although on one occasion my ego was to take a dent for our over-indulgence with a Chinese tourist who was told that we were still at war with the English, and that we stood guard just in case an attack was imminent. He looked confused as he left, but he got his own back when the picture he took of me and my cohorts appeared on the front cover of a Chinese gay porn magazine.

That coming summer, the castle was preparing for the Edinburgh Tattoo, a big mainly military parade, with many different bands, processions and events. A huge stand is erected every year in the castle esplanade, with small offices and studio boxes around the top of it.

Messing around with my muckers one evening, we made our way into one of the studios and found the controls for all the lighting and speakers. Like kids at Christmas, we started to play with the lights – fading up and down, turning on and off – and we talked into microphones in different voices. Trying to outdo my mates, and with my best Darth Vader impression, I bellowed out 'Luuuuuuke, I am your faaaaather!'

I soon found out to my horror that my friend had heard it from below in the esplanade, about 300 metres away. When he eventually found me, he told me that I'd been on a loudhailer system going out to the main high street in Edinburgh, and that I'd just pitched the whole of the castle into darkness.

Suffice to say that I didn't get much sleep that night, scrubbing and polishing the entire castle from top to bottom.

Experiences, positive or negative are valuable. We can learn from both, and they shape us in how we feel or act in the future. We can't change the past, but we can use them as a rudder to guide our future.

THE FIRST OF FOOT

The Royal Scots were the oldest and most senior infantry regiment in the British Army. Founded in 1633, by long tradition they took the front and right-hand side of the battlefield, a position that made them more commonly known as the 'first of foot, right of line'. The regiment had a long and proud history, and when you join an outfit steeped in such a history you hope to carry forward the fighting spirit of the men who went before you. Their name has changed many times as units have been reformed and they amalgamated with the King's Own Scottish Borderers to become simply 1 Scots in 2006, and then eventually becoming the Ranger Battalion around 2021.

As a youngster I shied away from politics, which I saw as grownups' affairs that held little interest for me. The day would come, however, when the special decisions announced would mean a great deal both to me and to all my comrades. The government's decision to restructure the British Army wouldn't apply to my battalion alone: its ripple effect would be felt by most infantry battalions, as the Scots division would see the loss of historic names including the Black Watch, the Argyll and Sutherland Highlanders and the Royal Highland Fusiliers.

The then secretary of state for defence, Geoff Hoon, would announce in December 2004 that all the main Scottish regiments were to amalgamate into one big regiment, namely the Royal Regiment of Scotland, which would be made up of six battalions and one company. The Royal Scots would merge with the King's Own Scottish Borderers to form the 1st Battalion, and other regiments would form the other battalions. The only things to be salvaged were the battalion tartan, stable belt and the glengarry, our traditional headdress, along with the differing colours of the hackles worn on the tam-o'-shanter.

When it happened I felt extremely pained by it all, and wondered what would become of the history, and the memory of the blood shed by members of these fiercely proud battalions during the two world wars and before.

In the mid-1990s all that was still in the future, but the problem of dwindling numbers and the difficulty in retaining soldiers that would eventually lead to the cuts were already being felt, so in the face of adversity we were sent on recruiting drives. It was a serious matter, but I still have to smile at the memory of one such event that quickly turned into a farce.

It was planned as an abseil to raise money and to potentially encourage new recruits who we hoped would be impressed when they saw how cool it was to be a soldier. Carrying a gun and abseiling down a large office block in Livingston, life could not be cooler – or so I thought.

An early-morning arrival of eager-beaver soldiers carried harnesses and ropes up onto the roof and, looking very professional, our small group quickly achieved the first desired aim and began to attract a crowd who watched in fascinated anticipation.

As we reached the summit of the building, I heard one joker among us ask, 'Any of you cunts done this before?' There was no response, and I realised that no, none of us had done this before.

With an air of negativity threatening to overshadow our valiant attempts to save our already doomed identity, the platoon sergeant got a grip on things. Rallying the troops, he ordered the youngest private soldier in the troop to don a harness and tentatively attached a rope.

Like unschooled infants, we looked on as he tried the harness first one way and then another, finally settling on something that resembled the sort of straitjacket Sir Anthony Hopkins might have worn in his role as a cannibal serial killer. He continued to fanny about before tying a big double bow onto the rope, so that he looked like a maniac in a camper-than-Christmas bondage outfit.

The sergeant ordered the rest of us to 'take a big handful of rope and lower him off the roof'. Thinking back, I recall being very aware that it didn't look or feel right, and those thoughts were confirmed when our volunteer realised that his trusted granny knot was slipping through his harness which, inevitably, was on upside down.

As the horror unfolded, the junior soldier began to scream and tried to pull himself back up onto the roof, but our sergeant, already committed, told us to keep on lowering him.

Worse was to come as our terrified 'volunteer', convinced he was about to plummet to his death, promptly wet himself. Eventually, we were told to haul him back up onto the roof, where, to the disbelief of every man there, our sergeant proceeded to beat the private up for 'cowardice' before calling for his next victim.

One of the guys made the mistake of piping up and saying, 'I've seen this done before.' He reckoned it was better if you went down forwards, or 'commando' style as he called it. Within minutes he was fitted up *Silence of the Lambs*-style, looking sharp on the edge of the rooftop, and just like before, we started to lower him.

The crowd below must surely by now have been anxious, and they would have been right to be. Suddenly our new volunteer looked awkward and uncomfortable and told us to lower him faster, which seemed like a strange thing to say.

Whether his request got lost in translation or his comrade was paying no attention, the guy with the first coil of rope just let go!

Our 'commando' rapidly disappeared from view and, as the slack was taken up by the fast-falling abseiler, the second coil nearly took one of the unharnessed guys who was holding it over the edge. Luckily, for his sake and for his abseiling mate's, he clung on, but suffered nasty rope burns for his efforts.

Daring to take a look over the edge, I could see that our once keen 'commando' was now unconscious, with blood trickling from a sizeable gash to the head. As he was lowered slowly to the ground, much to the shock and horror of the onlooking public, the police were called, and our recruitment team was removed from the building.

Suffice to say, no new recruits were found, and we did nothing to save our battalion later being absorbed into the new regiment, or to stop its name being lost for ever.

'It is not the strongest of the species that survives,
nor the most intelligent that survives.
It is the one that is most adaptable to change.'

Charles Darwin

JOCKS ON TOUR

Historically, infantry battalions train for war in various countries all around the world, using vast areas of ground that offer different climates and terrains. Cyprus was the first that I visited and, ironically, it offered a dusty, sweltering, desert environment – a climate I would grow all too familiar with, and one that would play a major part in how my military life would unfold and ultimately end. 'Lion Sun' was an infantry skills exercise designed to test soldiers in just this kind of hot and arid environment. Stepping from the plane on arrival, I was struck at once by the temperature difference. It was stifling.

No time for a sunshine break. Next morning, we were straight into acclimatisation training, steady-state jogging along the dusty tracks as the sun came up. The military skills routines were repetitive and hard going in the heat, and a lot of the guys, fair-haired and not used to such temperatures, suffered with sunburn.

During our time there, there was a television programme called *Soldier Soldier* starring Robson Green and Jerome Flynn. It was a show based on army life and they happened to be out in Cyprus filming and they asked for extras. My mates and I volunteered immediately and ended up being on the episode. I can be seen in a few scenes and firing an LSW (light support weapon) out of the window. We were even paid £50 for the day if I recall, which bought a few beers back then down in Limassol during R and R!

It was a shock to no one, but it turned into a harsh few weeks for some. I was glad when the exercise finished, and a well-earned day off turned into three days off as news came through that the battalion admin bods had forgotten to book return flights.

We were banned from hitting the tourist spots, so a few of us chipped in our money and hired a jeep to drive into a town that wasn't out of bounds. The heat ensured that most of us were parched, and not just for lack of water, so our money didn't stretch far.

Then one of our motley crew appeared from the back entrance to a hotel after relieving himself against a fire-exit door and then relieving the hotel of a crate of beer. On further investigation we found that most of the hotels had a small shed round the back of them which contained their reserve supplies of beer. Epic fail, Cyprus! We spent the night procuring crates at each hotel and then sat by their pools chatting up their guests until we were asked to leave. Our ingenuity worked well for the three days, and it felt like a mini-holiday before heading back to Blighty.

Next up, we visited Kenya for a bush exercise designed to test our resources in a jungle environment, although when we arrived at the jungle, called Kathendini, it was more of a sparse wood. After endless days as a boy foraging around woods with my dog, I felt comfortable in this terrain.

I was chosen to help out with the instructors this time, and the routine started with me meeting the blokes as they arrived and then assisting with taking them through basic jungle warfare training before setting them off on patrol.

As the days began to merge into one, the final ambush scenarios were soon upon us. The commander of the patrol would lay his men down in position, giving them arcs of fire to cover and brief orders, and they would then wait for nightfall and the arrival of the 'enemy', who in this case were remote-controlled targets.

During the initiation phase of the ambush, the commander was instructed to pat the two machine gunners either side of him to prompt them to spring the attack. As DS, or directing staff, we would normally supervise setting the ambush, and then disappear back to base, only to return some time later in the early hours of the morning to manipulate the targets.

During one scenario, just as it was starting to get dark, we left the set ambush in position before making our way back down the hill, but less than half an hour later all hell broke loose as the sound of gunfire echoed through the night like a thunderstorm. As we raced back up the hill, I wondered what the guys were firing at, seeing as we weren't due to put up the targets for another six hours.

When we got there, we could hear shouting, but the firing had died down. We found the young officer in charge, looking flushed amid all the smoke, and when asked what had happened he admitted that, as darkness fell, he had felt something moving around on his legs, and had looked down to see a pair of bright eyes looking back at him.

Startled, he'd grabbed hold of the guy sitting next to him, who had taken this as the sign to start the ambush and opened fire. In turn, and not to be outdone, the gunner sitting on the other side of the officer had opened fire himself, at which point the whole company had joined in, blazing away in all directions.

When the smoke cleared it was absolute carnage and there were holes all over. Trees had been shot down, and right in front of where the officer had been sitting was the bullet-riddled carcass of a hefty rat.

Looking at each other and looking at the slaughtered rodent, the silence was suddenly filled with laughter, and the taunting of the young officer went on long into the night. Fire-control orders began to be called like, 'COMPANY... ONE METRE... RATTUS RATTUS... RAPID FIRE!'

Our battalion's travels continued, and our next exercise was in Washington, in the US. We were sent to Yakima Ranges, and like idiots we packed shorts and suntan cream, thinking that we were heading to Washington DC. Where we were going, however, in Washington state on the other side of America, the temperatures were dropping to 30 degrees below.

I was sent to work with the range team, which meant more freedom and responsibility, something I enjoyed. My job this time was to supervise the attacking section as they advanced on a target and to move forward with the pair who would eventually be posting grenades in the enemy bunker. I had the responsibility of giving them a grenade already primed so that they could practise the final assault in gradual stages.

On a different task, but equally important, was Karchy, who was a good lad, but far from the sharpest tool in the box. He was assigned to monitor the fire-support group, who would keep the bunker under fire until we got close, at which point he would have them switch their fire in a safe direction. Textbook stuff, this practice was not difficult; it had been done by many before us, and no doubt would be done by many after.

In one particular scenario my assaulting pair were drawing near to the bunker, and as I walked behind the crawling grenadiers, I noticed some rounds bouncing off the sandbags directly in front of us. I stopped the grenadiers in their tracks and looked up to see why the fire support were still firing. What I saw was that Karchy was bird watching!

Having placed my approaching pair safely under cover, I sprinted to Karchy's position before he even noticed, and got his men to check their fire before getting stuck into him. 'You are a fucking arsehole, Karchy', I told him, and some more choice words for extras.

After that, the sergeant running the range decided to move Karchy away and keep him at the ammunition point, where he was to prepare all the weapons and grenades for the day's range.

Day two, and I set off again with my posting pair. Karchy handed me my grenades, which I put into the pocket of my smock. All was well as we made our approach. The grenadier was in position, so I stopped and took a grenade from my pocket. My heart then missed a beat when the body of the grenade dropped straight out of my hand, leaving me holding just the fly-off lever.

My life flashed before my eyes, and everything seemed to go in slow motion as I shouted, 'GRENADE!' as loud as I could and jumped onto the back of the shocked grenadier, who looked like he was ready to shit himself. Then, silence. Both of us froze.

Time passed. We waited and waited. No bang, no nothing. What had happened? I cautiously raised my head and looked in the direction of the grenade but couldn't see it. 'It must have been a dud', I thought to myself. 'What a stroke of luck.'

Moving gingerly to my feet, I spotted the grenade, and as I studied it I noticed that the detonator wasn't in the grenade and was still attached to the fly-off lever. 'Karchy!' I yelled. The grenade hadn't even been primed properly. Karchy must have just put the detonators straight into the hole of the grenades without screwing them home. I didn't know whether to laugh or cry.

The thing is, all battalions have men like Karchy, who was completely unaware of the ripple effect of his mistakes and that he'd just succeeded in knocking a year or two off my life.

But the drama didn't end there, and what happened next made Karchy's fuckups appear tame. At the end of the exercise, we were given a night off, and like clockwork we headed to the nearest town and the nearest pub or place that sold alcohol. Some really bad line dancing followed, and at the end of the night we all piled into taxis before heading back to camp.

Finnie, one of the lads in our car, for some reason decided to steal the taxi driver's pistol from under his seat, and without warning and much to everyone's surprise, he produced it back in the barrack block and started to wave it around while quoting from various cowboy films. Meanwhile, the taxi driver must have called the police, and it wasn't long before our block was surrounded by MPs, or Military Police.

They shouted through a loudhailer that everyone apart from Finnie was to exit the block, and a mad dash for the door ensued as everyone bolted out. Once outside we were lined up and searched, and then made to wait in the cold next to the corner of the block that now housed only Finnie and the pistol.

The loudhailer was used again, this time instructing Finnie to come out of the building with his hands raised, but there was no answer. The next message told him that he had five minutes to extract himself or they were going to storm the block.

At this point Finnie's face appeared at one of the windows and he shouted, 'I'm coming out and I'm coming out firing!'

'For fuck's sake!' we all gasped, but by some twist of fate we spotted him jumping out of the toilet window nearest to us before the MPs did. As he fell onto the ground outside the window, completely naked, three of us ran over and dived on top of him, followed quickly by the MPs who, with their weapons still drawn, ordered us to 'step back'.

After they saw he was unarmed, he was cuffed and dragged away. Finnie was locked up in the local town jail, and after what had turned into an international incident, he was later kicked out of the British Army, but it could have been terminally worse for him.

Perspective has always been important to me. It has always helped me keep balanced. We are products of our environment, which may seem obvious but as we grow up its our family unit, then school, work and television and social media, perhaps even travel. That's what gives us our values, beliefs, what is good or bad, right or wrong. Whether we are having a good day or bad day, essentially our *perspective*. But its only as good as our perspective and if we allow ourselves to expand that perspective we can see then maybe we're not having such a bad day and maybe things aren't as bad as we think.

> *'There is no elevator to success,*
> *you have to take the stairs.'*
>
> Zig Ziglar

THE LARDER MAN

With time moving on, I almost forgot the near misses we'd run into on exercise, and as I looked forward to another operational tour it was no surprise to me that Northern Ireland had made its way back onto the whiteboard in Battalion HQ.

The Royals were indeed being sent back to 'bandit country' in South Armagh. I'd got bored in the months leading up to deployment, so I was happy that this tour had the potential to be very different from the last.

During pre-deployment training the battalion ran a cadre for those who wished to join what was known as the COP or Close Observation Platoon. Across the water in Armagh, these shadowy guys stayed on the top floor of a base in Bessbrook Mill. You would rarely see them, and it was rumoured that they worked as close to Special Forces work as you could get in the green army.

If things worked out how I hoped, this would be my first look at the fabled men from Hereford who were the stuff of legend after recent successful ops in Gibraltar and Loughgall. Happily, I was selected to attempt the COP course, and after six weeks of intense fitness work and sleep deprivation I passed and became 2IC, or second-in-command of a patrol aged just 20.

As expected, the tour was much better than my last, and I thrived in the role that the COP played. We would collate intelligence through observation posts or take over watchtowers and use them with far better imaging equipment than that available to the green army.

Occasionally we would be in plain clothes, driving along roads that I'd only ever dared to tread in uniform on a patrol with heavy numbers. We were also given access to information that we would never have been allowed to know in normal circumstances, and were privy to intelligence about terrorist behaviour, along with knowledge of their future intentions or actions. We were trusted, and the responsibility gave me a sense of purpose and pride.

In the COP our tasks were a different type of routine. On an uneventful day or week, we stuck to the basic tasks required of a COP platoon – deploying at night; finding a bush or hide that overlooked a suspected terrorist's house and laying up for a week or two; using high-powered cameras and surveillance equipment to observe and log the suspect's movements and actions.

These methods provided vital intelligence that could later be used if one of the many agencies working in Northern Ireland were putting in a hard arrest, or a strike to counter a potential terrorist attack. The work wasn't glamorous, but it was rewarding and seemed to offer more results than overt patrols did.

In a typical hide there would be four of us, side by side, up close and personal. We would do everything in front of each other, and 'everything' included minute attention to detail. If it went into your body, you carried it; if it came out of your body you carried it.

One particular night, 'Mids' had just come off stag, and he woke me because it was my turn to stand watch, or lie on watch, to be precise. I rolled over him and assumed the position on sentry duty.

Along with monitoring the camera I looked for anything else that might hold strategic importance. Barely a minute had passed before Mids turned to me, eyes bulging from his skull in panic, 'Col, quick, the Clingfilm!'

Mids, as it turned out, had no time for such niceties. He couldn't get his position right or his trousers down quick enough and emptied his arse of diarrhoea little more than three inches from my face. The shite splattered everywhere, including my face, and the smell was unbearable.

This wasn't the cool spy role that I'd envisaged. Several wet wipes later I saw the funny side, but thoughts of a life in Her Majesty's Special Forces couldn't have been further from my mind that night.

The tour flew by. I had embraced a different type of soldiering and yearned for more of it, so I started to spend more time in the gym, building up my physical fitness, knowing that, during the types of scenarios I craved, mental and physical stamina were a must.

But not all my thoughts were directed towards 'sneaky-beaky' ops. Like most men who serve, I enjoyed the distraction of many attractive women, and my bed space had a small board next to it covered with pictures of long-distance admirers, or pen pals, that I had acquired.

One of the lads joked, 'You could make your own men's magazine out of those, Col.' I mentioned this to one particular admirer, and jokingly told her that I'd sent her picture into a men's mag. The next day she told me that she had done the same with one of my pictures! Laughs all round, until a month later my photograph was on the centre-page spread of a British tabloid titled 'Hunk of the Month'. Not the best way to win friends and influence people in the world of clandestine operations.

The tour passed peacefully, and every man looked forward to some post-tour leave. First up was the usual muckers' holiday, and then I decided to break with tradition and go home. I pulled up outside, stepped cautiously out of the car, and took a big lungful of air before I headed in and searched for signs of life.

At first I was taken aback, because the home of two cottages knocked into one that I had left was now restored to two separate living spaces. It turned out that my mum had split from my stepfather, who was now living in one side while my mother was occupying the other side with her new lover.

Unfortunately, what with me being away, my younger brother and sisters had borne the brunt of this split, and after many arguments and disputes, my stepfather would eventually have to go to court to gain custody of my younger siblings – a case that he thankfully won.

Looking back now, I'm glad I made the effort to go home. I couldn't just turn my back on my past life, which is what I would have done if it were not for my little brother and sisters. I worried about them and didn't want to lose touch, and it has turned out to be for the best.

When we returned from leave the pace slowed somewhat as we embraced another mundane shift of public duty, this time as the Royal Guard at Balmoral Castle. We became the 'pony platoon', and our job was to accompany foreign dignitaries and visiting royal families around the vast highland estate.

We would often help during shoots, manoeuvring the culled deer with the help of ponies down to the nearest road and onto a Land Rover, where they would be whisked away to the local larder for skinning and butchering. My own role within this well-oiled machine came with a name: 'The Larder Man'.

Resenting the title at first, along with the idea of working in a glorified cupboard, I was relieved to learn that 'The Larder Man' role was far from the stores. I embraced the responsibility of being first into work, and much of my day was spent outside skinning the heads of the stags that I'd left in the heavy cast-iron boiling pot from the night before.

I would shine the items that emerged, made up of a set of antlers and the crown of the skull. When finished, some would take pride of place on a budding huntsman's mantelpiece. The others were given as gifts at the end of the hunt season, with the very best, or pieces that consisted of twelve or more points, ending their days on the walls of the palace itself.

Once all tasks were complete, usually before lunchtime, I would content myself with an afternoon of PT or golf on the course in the castle grounds, though my enthusiasm for the game diminished fast when one particularly wayward drive crashed through a couple of horse riders, the ball narrowly missing my own colonel-in-chief Queen Elizabeth II. My feeble attempts to cry 'Fore!' had been lost in the wind.

In the late afternoon the lads would arrive at intervals with a stag or two. They had already been gutted, so the stomachs had been removed and all the blood drained from the bodies to preserve the meat. I would then skin them, which was relatively quick while they were still warm, and cut off the hooves and head before hanging them in the freezer, prepped and ready either to be sold to the local butchers or to end up as venison in the royal kitchen. Like most young soldiers, I never tired of the fact that the genitals were kept and sold separately as a delicacy to the Asian community, and still laugh now at the banter we had about it.

Those days are remembered fondly. I enjoyed the freedom and responsibility I had in the larder, and there was fun to be had around the castle.

Our platoon sergeant (Sneds) wasn't immune to the banter either, and he decided one day to play a trick on our naïve young platoon commander, who was fresh out of the factory. Concocting a plan, he said, 'Col, dive in the freezer for a second and pretend to be having your way with one of the stags. I want to see if this lad has a sense of humour.'

I agreed, laughing, before making my way into the large freezer. A few minutes later there was a knock on the wall of the freezer, and I took this as my cue to start my sex scene. I pulled my trousers down and grabbed the stag, which was hanging upside down and looking less than attractive, and so the show began.

There was a second knock on the wall of the freezer, this time much louder, so I continued with my motion. The door slowly opened as I stifled my laughter for what seemed an eternity. I heard my platoon sergeant's voice and then, as I threw myself into my acting with increased enthusiasm, I heard words that will haunt me for ever: 'The larder, Your Highness.'

Looking up in horror, I locked eyes with my platoon sergeant, who gestured for me to stop with a flat hand across his throat. I dived to pull up my trousers, and no sooner had I done so than my new platoon commander crossed the threshold with His Royal Highness Prince Philip.

Sweating in a freezer, I stood to attention, trying hard to ensure that the rising tide of nausea did not overwhelm me. *What the fuck?* I thought. 'Hello, so you're The Larder Man', said the Duke of Edinburgh, extending his hand to meet mine. 'Er, yes sir, that's me', I stammered back, looking in disbelief at my platoon sergeant, who was now smiling with relief.

I proceeded to show the duke around as he asked the usual questions about where I grew up and my life in the army thus far. Saying goodbye, he left with the platoon commander, who was still oblivious to the whole thing.

I turned to my sergeant in shock, and he just slumped to the floor with a sigh. 'I had no idea', he said. 'I tried to warn you by banging on the wall when he arrived.' A moment of belly laughter followed, and my sergeant then pointed to my fly zip, which had been down, and gaping open the whole time. Sneds was a great character and I ended up in his team in Northern Ireland and we played tennis together. He died far too soon after leaving the army and my old unit holds an annual golf day in his memory.

That near-calamity aside, the tour couldn't have gone better, and concluded with a final party, which was called the Ghillies Ball, after all the ghillies, or gamekeepers, on the royal estate. Many of the royal family were present, so it was quite a moment for a young man from such a broken background.

I was awarded best pony man for my efforts as The Larder Man, which was all the more amazing because no larder man had won it before, and it usually went to one of the guys who went up the hills with the guests. I was very proud of that award as voted by the gamekeepers of Balmoral, who were good, honest, hard-working people. My name is still engraved on the cup today.

The company was given a long weekend after that, and being rather short of funds, we came up with a plan to make ourselves some spending money. We decided to dress up in our Royal Scots uniform and go into Edinburgh high street 'fund raising'.

We managed to get some new-looking buckets and covered them in stickers from the recruiting office, and then four of us paraded up and down Princes Street. We did very well, and so decided to spread our wings and headed up the Royal Mile and towards the castle.

At the foot of the castle is the esplanade, which was full of visitors, so we ventured in warily, weaving our way through the crowds, me chuckling to myself at the weight of my now heavy bucket. My heart stopped, however, as the crowd parted before me and my very own commanding officer appeared, getting out of a staff car in front of the castle gates.

I tried to spin around, but it was too late. He had caught sight of me and bellowed, 'Lance Corporal, over here!' My stomach churned. All that time and effort and money raised was going to be for nothing, and I'd probably wind up in jail now.

'Wouldn't be setting much of an example if I didn't contribute, would I?' he said, and put a crisp five-pound note into my bucket. I didn't know whether to laugh or cry, having gone from a lengthy jail sentence to being paid a fiver by my very own CO in the space of two minutes.

I decided I'd ridden my luck far enough, and gathered the rest of the lads, who would never have believed me if one of them hadn't witnessed the whole thing from his hiding place behind one of the statues. We went back to Princes Street, cashed the money in at the bank, and decided to hand half of it into the recruiting office and keep the other half as 'wages' for our work. Well, at least until pay day, when we paid it all back. It was a fruitful weekend.

The Royal Scots had finished their tour of Inverness and were now being posted to Colchester, a garrison town in Essex. We had a totally different job now, being part of the new concept of an Airmobile Brigade. Colchester had several regiments in residence, including separate Engineers and Signals. The military jail was also in Colchester, where the more serious offenders spent their time and always seemed to come out much fitter than when they went in.

Essex has its own reputation for scantily clad women, so I enjoyed my time there. One of the first women I got acquainted with turned out to be the daughter of a serving RSM.

As it goes, I have never been especially successful with relationships, but it's never been through a lack of the will to try. One Sunday, I was invited to this young lady's house for dinner. I tried to decline the offer, but she insisted that it was on her father's orders, so I foolishly agreed.

I dressed smartly, I watched my manners at the table, and although I was a nervous wreck, it seemed to pass OK. Her father said we should retire to the conservatory for cheese and biscuits. That wasn't something I was used to, but I followed them in, looking forward to the end of a successful evening.

I asked her father where the bathroom was before making my way to it. 'Top of the stairs on the left-hand side', he explained.

I got into the bathroom and having had quite a big lunch, used the toilet to full effect, whereupon my physical relief morphed into mental torture when the flush decided not to work. After pushing several times to no avail, I started to panic. This was not the impression I had hoped to leave.

Grabbing the toilet brush, I tried to break up the unwanted tenant, but still had no joy. Aware of how long I had been away by now, desperate thoughts began to run through my head, and finally, in full panic mode, I grabbed some toilet paper, seized and wrapped the offending article, and launched it, javelin style, through the narrow side window of the bathroom.

Mission accomplished; I scrubbed my hands before rushing downstairs. I sat down with the rest of the household and was aware at once of an eerie silence. I glanced across to my girlfriend, and she motioned skywards with her eyes.

I followed where I thought she was looking, only to spy a parcel covered in flapping toilet paper balanced precariously on the glass roof of the conservatory. Within minutes I found myself in the back seat of a taxi, which had been kindly booked for me, carrying my unwanted guest. Needless to say, that was another relationship that didn't last.

Both the Queen and Sneds, my old sergeant, are no longer with us so enjoy the special moments you have. They never last forever and all you have is your memories. The good times.

GLADIATOR READY!

After another twelve-month training cycle, the battalion was sent to Northern Ireland again. Being in the Recce Platoon, I was to be a part of the COP for the tour's duration, and I was reminded briefly of Mids-gate as I packed my kit and equipment.

Looking back, this was a phase in my life that may have changed its course for ever. 'A reason for everything, for everything a reason' they say, and it applied to my life at this point. I had been watching *Soldier, Soldier* on the telly and it had given me an appetite for getting involved in TV.

I had also been watching *Gladiators* when an advert came up asking for members of the public to apply. I jotted down the address, sent off for the paperwork, and when it arrived, filled it in without much thought and sent it back.

I then pushed it to the back of my mind as I began my tour, but a few months in I received a letter from the producers saying I had been picked to come and compete in the trials for the upcoming TV show. I was overjoyed with the gobbing-off rights and showed it gleefully around the platoon.

My immediate superiors were far less impressed, and I feared that I wouldn't be allowed to take part, as it was during our tour, but luckily the adjutant saw a niche and thought this could be the answer to our recent recruiting problem, what with the media attention I might receive.

He told me that they would pay for my flight home as long as I qualified, but if I didn't then I must pay for it myself. No pressure,

Right: Me and my brother John and sisters Jane and Sarah.

Below: End of Depot training as a 15-year-old.

Guarding Edinburgh Castle.

Above left: 1RS Infantry football champions.

Above right: Welterweight boxing champion.

The Macmafia (Del, Frank, Me, Stevie and Tam Gow MM).

Above left: I always had to stay flexible in the army!

Above right: The Queen's Butcher at Balmoral.

Graduating First Class with my little helper son Darius.

Training is great for the mind and body and these days I stretch more!

Above left: In Combats, Who Dares Stares!

Above right: Army days as a recce team commander.

Left: Motion capture for film and games at Pinewood Studios near the 007 hangar.

Above: Mocap for video games.

Right: Channel 4's SAS: Who Dares Wins.

ITV's This Morning.

Bear Grylls and me.

Right: Who Dares Cares doing the Kiltwalk.

Below: Nepal post-earthquakes for the NSPCC.

Black tie awards.

Above left: Public Speaking.

Above right: Headshot for acting/motion capture credits.

then! I wasn't sure if I could afford the fare, but I agreed, and two weeks later I was on my way home.

The trials took place in the Meadowbank stadium, an indoor athletics arena in Edinburgh. I'd been training quite hard in Northern Ireland, and thought I was relatively fit as an all rounder. On arrival, though, I saw that the place was full of all shapes and sizes, from marathon runners to bodybuilders, and I felt quite small and puny compared with some of them.

Once I had handed in my name, I was given a time to appear for my trial, and I sat down to watch the proceedings. Eventually, I was called forward and found myself with nine other guys all hoping to make it through.

We started on a running machine and had to run 800 metres in two minutes, a brisk pace that deselected two or three guys. Filling in the paperwork was the easy part. Moving on, we were instructed to do twenty controlled pull ups, go straight into a monkey-bar crossing, and then do a 25-feet rope climb twice in a minute.

All this was pretty challenging, and by the end of it there were only two of us left. The final event we were given was called the pugil-stick fight, which involved wielding a thick staff with a large pad at either end, and the idea was to knock your opponent out of a marked circle.

I had to defend for thirty seconds, attack for thirty seconds, then we both had to attack for thirty seconds. During the last phase I managed to knock the helmet off the other guy, who I had noticed was wearing a tight white vest with a red trim, the uniform of the PTI, or physical training instructors, of the British Army. I wasn't about to be beaten by another soldier!

After the trial I was asked to stay behind and was given a time to go in for an interview. When my time came, I entered a small office where a camera was set up with two or three people sitting opposite asking questions, mainly about my background. They explained that they wanted to see how I was in front of the camera, encouraging me to speak in a natural way, and asked if I had any funny stories.

With unpleasant images of Mids flashing through my mind, I knew that most of my army stories wouldn't go down well with this audience, so I explained that I'd come from Northern Ireland and that we didn't have too much in the way of comedy out there, but I did have one amusing tale to tell from a time I was home on annual leave.

I had ventured out one night in a particularly rough area of Edinburgh, and as usual I was driving. I wouldn't class myself as teetotal, but I was generally the one who didn't drink.

I parked the car outside the house of a girl whose acquaintance I had made earlier, but she advised me that it was a bad area and that my car would be vandalised. I assured her that I was planning to leave early in the morning and that it should be OK.

Next morning, up bright and early, I peered out of the curtains to see that my car was still parked where I had left it. Feeling relieved, I said my farewells and left the house, but when I got round to the driver's side of the car I could see that the window had been smashed and my stereo stolen.

'For fuck's sake!' I thought. Gutted and a little embarrassed at having been so cocksure of myself, I took the car to a local garage and got the window fixed. I didn't have the cash for a new stereo, so I put that thought on the back burner.

A couple of nights later, I found myself at the same address being given the same warnings as before. I insisted that there was nothing worth stealing, now that my stereo had been taken, but to ease her mind I placed an A4 piece of paper in the window stating that there were no valuables in the car as the stereo had already been stolen.

Same ritual as before. I wake up, see my car sitting where I'd parked it, leave the house, walk around to the driver's side, and see … that the window has yet again been smashed!

Only this time, with black humour and time on their hands, the culprits had placed a banner of their own in the window saying,

'JUST CHECKING!' It felt like a scene from the film *Trainspotting*. If it hadn't been my car it would have been hilarious.

After the interview I was told that they would be in touch, so I returned to my unit to tell them that I had successfully passed the trials and that I was waiting to see if I'd been picked to appear on the show, happy in the knowledge that I wouldn't have to fund my own trip.

I received a letter around three or four weeks later saying I had been picked as a reserve on the show and that I had to turn up in Birmingham to go through all the events. I turned up as requested and was pleased to beat the then record for the eliminator assault course. As things turned out, the guy who I was reserve for didn't qualify, so that was the end of my next shot at TV stardom. It's funny now seeing *Gladiators* back on the television.

Back to battalion life, I concentrated on my army career, which, on a lighter note, included playing as striker or left wing for the battalion football team. To be honest, I was only a fringe player, but I like to think I did my bit, as we won the Infantry Cup.

My physical fitness was top notch, and I felt that I was gathering good soldiering experience at every turn. Frustration had begun to kick in on base though, as the long queue of people lining up for the promotion ladder grew longer still, with certain rungs causing problems for those ahead.

There were several guys older than, or senior to, me who were struggling to pass the SCBC (Section Commander's Battle Course). It was hard to have to watch them missing out without being given a shot myself because I was seen as too young.

I eventually chose to move to the Signals Platoon so that I could try for the SCBC as a member of HQ Company, and the tactic worked. I got on the course and passed, and then I passed the signals equivalent. Careerwise, this was a sideways step, but it helped me because I saw the infrastructure of the battalion and the bigger picture in terms of the battlefield, including the parts people played in the wartime role.

I finished my time in the signals and returned to the Recce Platoon. These are supposed to be the finest soldiers of any regiment, and although it's not always the case, we had a good mix in our platoon.

It was here that I met a couple of guys who had tried for SAS selection. I knew nothing about the SAS, aside from the stories that went around, but Cookie and Eddie knew about the selection process. The fact that they had failed was quite daunting, as they were switched-on soldiers, very fit and keen, and both well respected and experienced in the battalion.

One of them had lasted around two months, the other three. No Royal Scots were serving in the SAS at the time, so it looked to be a bit of a challenge, and no wonder. The SAS was regarded as the most elite unit in the world, the model for all other elite units the world over. They were the trailblazers for clandestine operations, so I decided to apply.

My application to leave the Royal Scots was not looked on favourably by all within the command elements of the regiment. My friends and the Officer Commanding were keen, but not many people at the top level were. They were reluctant to see another man leave when recruiting and retention were at an all-time low.

Promoted to corporal and asked by the CO if I wished to consider a career as an officer in the regiment, I declined, much to the dismay of my grandmother. I was made PMC (President of the Mess Committee) of the Corporals' Mess, and I was sent down on the recce commander's course.

I enjoyed the challenge and passed, but something was missing. I had far too much drive for the time I was spending in rank, and I felt I was being held back from something far greater. I was hungry.

I found out through a friend in the admin office that my paperwork to apply for SAS selection had mysteriously ended up in the shredder, so I made sure that it was resubmitted as I stood there, watching the fax for myself. I eventually received paperwork back from Hereford giving me a place and a date to turn up.

Don't have regrets about wishing you had given something a go or missed opportunities. Just give it a go, what's the worst that could happen. At least you'll know, and not knowing or having regrets lasts much longer.

'Perseverance is demonstrated by those who keep going when the going gets tough, who don't give up even when others say it can't be done.'

James E. Faust

SAS SELECTION

It was January and there was a hard frost on the ground when I turned up in Wales for the first phase of the famously brutal selection ordeal with two other guys from the Royal Scots.

One was a good friend, Chris, who had the lungs of a racehorse, had run for the army, and, before he joined, had cycled for Great Britain. The other guy, Willie, I knew less well. I had met him previously during a tour of Northern Ireland, and then again just before selection when he had come back from a posting. It was 1998 and he was steering his way around our base and had stopped to ask me for directions. After a while he recognised me from our first meeting and just said, 'Gee! They're making anybody up these days!' and drove off.

I had received a lot of negative vibes about selection, with everybody telling me how long they thought I would last and nobody giving me short odds on surviving to the end. I'll admit I could have been better prepared, but I knew little of selection, and though I knew I needed hill training there were none around Colchester. I had been given around a week off by my OC, a great guy called Guy Richardson who would later become Director of Operations for the British Lions. Unfortunately, it was about a fortnight before selection and so I used it to familiarise myself with the Brecon Beacons and Elan Valley, as I knew that most of the routes were in that area.

It wasn't until I arrived at Sennybridge camp that I bumped into another guy from the Royal Scots. He was an officer I had never met previously. He had been given about three months off to train. I was flabbergasted and not a little disgruntled at this unfair advantage. We said hello and then sat down to the opening brief and roll call. Looking around, there were loads of guys sitting in the mess hall, all hoping to complete the course, and it was quite daunting to see so many.

Like my mates back in my unit, I didn't fancy my odds on day one, as one of my friends had said less than 5 per cent pass, but I didn't know if that was true or not.

We had our names read out, and then the Chief Instructor stood up and told us how the next four weeks would run. First we would have some simple infantry-style tests, like military knowledge and map reading, and then we would go out and do a CFT, or Combat Fitness Test, which was an annual test for infantry and was pretty straightforward – 8 miles in two hours with your pack and rifle. I was surprised to see most of the groups complete in around an hour and a half.

Even at this early stage people were looking tired, and Willie was actually the last man in, only just making the time. It was to take its toll on him, and the very next day he was one of the first to drop out of the initial selection group. Over the next few days, we went out onto the hills in trekking groups where we would each take a leg of the route, map reading and leading the group. As the week wore on this evolved into doing long jogs in the morning and going out in the hills in the afternoon, with the groups getting smaller and smaller until we were in pairs.

For a 'winter' selection, the weather wasn't too bad in the Brecons, which can be treacherous at the best of times, with the weather changing from benign to lethal in the space of a few hours. It's no wonder that civilian walkers often get themselves into trouble in those hills, and there have unfortunately been a few guys over the years who have died on them while pushing themselves to their limit and beyond in a desperate bid to pass selection.

So, no snow yet, but I certainly knew I was in the depths of January as I climbed out of my maggot (army sleeping bag) after a seriously early reveille, still aching from the previous day's beasting, and made my way, shivering in the dark, from the ramshackle huts to the outside washrooms each morning.

We quickly fell into a routine of 4.30 am reveille; wash and shave and breakfast by 4.45 am; collect your weapon from the armoury at 5.00 am; then into the car park, fully kitted up, ready by 5.15 am to clamber aboard the 4-tonne trucks and be trundled off on a bumpy road trip for anything up to ninety minutes, depending where that day's exercise was being held.

For the early marches we had to carry anything upwards of 35 pounds in our bergens, not including water and food, which was nothing compared to the loads we would have to carry if we survived deep into this phase. Failure to complete any daily route meant you would be instantly off the course.

The first big milestone in our course came at the end of week one, as we tackled the so-called 'Fan dance'. This is a route march in sizeable groups over Pen y Fan, a large and notorious hill in the midst of the Brecon Beacons.

Reveille that morning was even earlier than usual, and there was another thick frost on the ground as we piled wearily into the trucks for a road journey that gave us plenty of time to wonder why the hell we were putting ourselves through this.

At the bottom of the course, with an immediate steep incline ahead of us, we were split into about five groups of thirty or so, each led by a DS member who set off at a relentlessly punishing pace as we jostled for the most advantageous position to clamber over the rough terrain behind him.

Scrabbling over the uneven turf and crumbling soil and rock, your face was often bumping into the fluorescent orange safety panel on the back of the bergen just in front of you, while the boots of the guy behind you, who was colliding with your own safety panel, were raking down the backs of your calves until you could fight your way into a bit of space.

The idea was never to be level with the DS, but about 5 or 10 metres behind. As the hill took its toll, that gap was bound to start to lengthen, with the stragglers up to a kilometre behind by the time the DS was nearing the peak of the 'Fan'.

We were told that the normal time allowed to do the course was around four hours, but you couldn't be sure. Rather like a golf tournament 'cut', the actual time allowed would depend on the weather and the average time taken by the whole cadre, so you couldn't afford to lag too far behind the DS, who was powering on ahead like some unstoppable machine.

With shoulders burning, legs screaming and lungs fit to burst, I reached the top of the 'Fan' to be greeted by another member of the Directing staff, snugly wrapped in a sleeping bag in his bivouac shelter, sipping from a steaming hot cup of tea, and he checked I knew which way I was headed before wishing me on my way with some gratuitously smart-arse comment.

I had no time to reflect on the spectacular view from the top before I was clambering down the suicidally steep incline known as Jacob's Ladder, with our DS pacesetter still in my sights but now some way ahead.

With a heavy pack on your back, the upper slope of the Ladder has, over the years, claimed plenty of casualties who didn't pick the right foothold, but though my knees were killing me with the strain of controlling my descent, I picked my way safely down the precipitous slope and pressed on to the long Roman road at the bottom of the U-shaped valley below.

By this stage the groups of guys were well strung out, but though I wasn't right up at the front, I was thankfully not lagging too far back.

The DS stepped up the pace even more along the ancient track, so that I was torn at times between fast walking and breaking into a jog. Neither choice was comfortable, but I just pressed on, stopping briefly to take on board water and food, knowing that at the turnaround point

I would have to double back and climb the Ladder again to the top of the 'Fan', and I would need all the energy inside me that I could get.

Some find scaling the top of the Ladder strangely easier than going down it, but there was nothing easy about the climb as far as I was concerned, and I was running on adrenalin to keep the pain at bay. Back at the peak once again, at least there was a feeling of relief that the worst of the route was behind me.

One more descent and another smaller climb before the final slope down to the finish, and though I might not be up with the DS when he reached the bottom, he was still in sight as I was running in, and, knowing how stretched out the guys behind me were, I felt confident that I'd beaten the cut-off time.

Those who hadn't would be off the course. Indeed, several more guys fell out at this stage, but there still seemed to be hundreds of us left.

The next few weeks were a variation on the same theme. We would wake up around 4.00 or 5.00 M in the morning, load up on breakfast calories as fast as we could, whether or not we felt hungry at that time of the morning, and then go and sit in the cold wet car park and wait for our names to be called out, whereupon we would load onto a truck and vanish off into the hills.

We would receive a time to report to the instructor at the front of the truck, and when our time came up we would be given a grid reference and told to indicate it on the map, then we would set off.

The general rule was to allow around 4 kilometres per hour, as the ground was steep and boggy and the going was slow. This was a brisk pace though, and you couldn't afford to stop or get lost.

We all had a certain amount of safety kit, which we had to take with us up into the hills, and our packs, which the DS would check for weight along the way, were by this stage, even without counting our water, loaded with around 50 pounds. On top of this we also had our rifles, which had to be carried with both hands at all times or you would be kicked off the course. We weren't allowed to walk on paths or tracks, and again, if caught, they'd kick you off the course, as some found to their cost.

Once we reached our assigned grid reference point, which was usually the peak of one of the many hills in the area, we would be given another grid reference and it would start all over again. We never knew when it would stop, or how far we'd have to go; we simply carried on until the instructor told us to get back on the truck.

After the day was completed, we would be driven back to the camp, fix our packs for the next day, dry out our clothes, shower and go for dinner. Then it was usually an early night, or on odd days as the course wore on I would go down to the gym, relax in the jacuzzi and then get a pizza on the way back.

After three weeks of this, and having seen the numbers on the course dwindle, we were told it was 'test week': the final week of the endurance phase, or 'hills phase' as we called it. This was a series of routes, especially difficult, that had to be completed to tight deadlines. Failure to complete one in the time stated meant a 'yellow card', and two yellow cards would ditch you from the course. If you failed to complete any route at any stage, you were also off the course.

To add to the hardship, the weather had now turned to blizzard conditions.

The wind whipped over the hilltops and sliced up through the valleys, driving the snow into your face. Not soft Alpine snow, but tiny chunks of ice that pebble dashed your skin and left it red and stinging. As the white storm descended you knew exactly why you had the fluorescent panel on the back of your bergen, though at just a few paces the bright orange disappeared from view, and on a couple of occasions some of us would be taken off the course by the DS to help look for other guys who had got lost in the white out!

I found one of these marches particularly gruelling. It was an agonising forced march across some of the toughest ascents and descents the Welsh hills have to offer, and the icy weather made it all the harder. Everyone is different, but for me it was more difficult than previous routes because there were more changes in elevation than on any of the others, and certainly more steep climbs.

As we bumped along in the dark in the 4-tonner on the way to this day's torture, the bitter wind cut through the canvas sides of the truck, which offered scant protection, but when we arrived at our destination and piled out, I longed for the warmth we'd just left.

I crouched on my bergen and clung to a last moment's rest before the ordeal ahead, until it was my turn to launch on the nightmare course. The DS called me forward and told me the grid reference of my first checkpoint before reminding me, as if I needed telling by now, not to use pathways or any tracks a vehicle could manage, and to hold my rifle in both hands at all times.

I found the reference quickly on my map, set the bearing on my compass and pointed with a gloved hand for the benefit of the DS the direction I was about to head off in.

'Go on then, Maclachlan, what are you waiting for?' he said. The high point on the map was around 7 kilometres away as the crow flies, but I was no crow, and between me and my destination was a large V-shaped valley that would take me at least an extra couple of kilometres to traverse.

I calculated it would take me around two hours to the top, but I was already falling behind on my timings by the time I struggled to the spot height where the first DS checkpoint was waiting.

My toes and fingers were numb from the cold, my breath was laboured, and it was all I could do to gasp, 'Maclachlan, Staff!' The DS gave me an indifferent glance and told me to point out on my map where we were. I pointed to the grid reference, willing him to give me a quick confirmation, but at the same time enjoying the brief rest while we went through this formality. 'Are you certain?' he said, trying to plant a seed of doubt in my mind. I was, and he gave me my next grid reference.

I repeated it back to him to be sure, and he had me point it out on the map.

'OK then, you'd better get on with it', he said as I placed my frozen fingers around a blade of grass and pointed to the spot.

I still had to make my way through the notorious, precipitous gorge through the landscape known as 'VW' valley, because of all the men who've found it a barrier too far to the completion of their selection dreams and have voluntarily withdrawn.

There were more climbs and descents even before I got there, and yet more after I somehow clambered and stumbled through the thick gorse and clumps of bog grass along the way to my next grid reference and the next unsympathetic DS.

Eventually, sodden wet, cold and exhausted, I reached the final checkpoint, praying that the DS waiting there would not give me a withering look and a new grid reference. Mercifully, he greeted me with a begrudging, 'Well done. Go and get in the lorry.'

My final report would later reveal that I had passed that one with only minutes to spare, narrowly avoiding a yellow card.

There was never a point when I felt like giving up or thought that I would fail, but nor was there any point when I thought I would pass. I just focused on getting through each day's ordeal and never looking any further ahead.

It was at the point-to-point stage that my friend Chris came off. He had fallen badly and hurt his back and was finding it hard to make the time. He eventually withdrew and was gutted, and I was gutted for him because if anything, this was his strong area and I had expected him to complete comfortably.

The arduous week pressed relentlessly on, and it concluded with a 70-kilometre, or 40-mile, endurance march. This had to be completed in twenty hours and was the final hurdle of this phase. We would be carrying a minimum of 55 pounds of weight in our bergens, not including water and rations, which could easily take the weight up to 90 pounds.

A good sleep beforehand was essential, but trying to sleep wasn't easy, what with the pain from blisters, shoulder sores and various other niggles, and knowing what was ahead of us.

Even before night had changed to early morning we were woken and had to force our aching muscles and rubbed-raw bodies out into the freezing January air to use the washroom toilets before we crammed more vital calories into ourselves at a late-night breakfast. We clambered once more into the trucks for the ominous journey to the place of our upcoming torture.

It was midnight, or not long after, when we were set off at intervals and eventually found ourselves in small groups trekking together over the course. I will always remember my legs feeling like jelly, and seeing a small, wiry, cheerful fellow called Dave, who was to remain my friend for years after, passing me on his way back from the halfway point when I still had a couple of kilometres to go! He was usually at the front and was as fit as a butcher's dog.

I found myself in a group with two other Scottish guys, one called Stu, who was a corporal in the Argyle and Sutherland Highlanders, and the other an officer called Murray, who had been posted to our admin office in the battalion several years before and who I knew was extremely fit.

As we hiked up and down the seemingly endless hills we bumped into the guy from the Royal Scots, and he seemed really tired. He suggested he join our group and asked me to help him. I agreed, and after a while we sat down for a quick lunch stop. We had only been sitting there for a few minutes when the Royal Scots guy suddenly said he was OK and set off on his own. That seemed strange, but I thought nothing of it until a few hours later when we came across a large taped-up parcel sitting on the grass at the bottom of a hill. Murray told me it was the Royal Scots guy's, and that he had been ditching his weight after his pack had been weighed in at certain checkpoints. I couldn't understand how he could gamble like this and think he would not be found out, but I just slogged on, waging my own personal battle against the gruelling route.

Exhausted, but with the end of the march close at hand, I was surprised to see another checkpoint just before the finish. I found out much later that the Royal Scots guy had been caught out here, and had been allowed to complete the phase, but was later pulled into the training officer's office and kicked off the course with a bad report.

The hills phase was complete, and to confirm it the instructors read out the names of those still left on the course. There were just forty-six remaining, and I was one of them. I was dog tired but pleased with myself and went up the road that weekend feeling proud I had lasted as long as I had.

I was to report to Hereford after the weekend off, and this was the first sight I had of Stirling Lines. This place, to me, had always been shrouded in mystery, and its occupants the subjects of many heroic tales. I found it strange, then, that this 'secret' base was in the middle of a residential estate. Inside, I had expected to find a hive of activity, with people busily preparing for secret missions or training on the latest James Bond gadgetry, but I was struck by how quiet it was.

Looking back now, I know that at any one time at least half the regiment could be overseas on operations or training; that the CT (counter-terrorism) team were probably at a training centre or waiting on standby at home; and that the rest were either at home or away on external courses. Very few men live in, on base, which would be the norm in many other units. If there were squadrons on base at the time, then we saw little of them, as we were placed in the transit accommodation, six or eight of us to a room.

We were now on the jungle phase and had to go through an induction package that would train us in patrolling, attacks and ambushes, setting up harbour positions, or just LUPs (Lay-Up Positions) where we could eat, rest or send comms scheds. After practising in our patrols, we set off for Brunei. I had never been to the jungle and was actually looking forward to it, but some of the guys were JWIs (Jungle Warfare Instructors) and knew exactly what to expect. These guys didn't look too thrilled!

For the first week we were in a small camp outside the jungle, close to the sea, and would be woken up early in the morning to go on long and tiring beach runs. The sand would really take it out of you and needed a very different kind of fitness from that required for scaling hills in the cold, wet climate of Wales. We would then go down to the ranges in the afternoon, and this was an arduous task in the extreme heat. We carried a lot of weight and would practise our drills over and over until it became second nature.

Eventually, we were flown into the jungle to start our full-on warfare training, and right away you felt the humidity under the canopy of the trees. I was struck by the constant background noise of animals, exotic birds and various unfamiliar creatures that filled this alien world, and the thick undergrowth that meant you could rarely see more than 20 metres ahead of you, so that for the next four weeks I would rarely see the sky.

We made A-frames to sleep in at night, and we would be up by first light to go to the schoolhouse to receive lessons from the instructors, then spend virtually all day getting more practical lessons, and in the evening noting down what we'd learned in our 'Jungle Books'.

The early days consisted mostly of ranges and patrols, but as time wore on this developed into a wartime scenario, and we would go out actively patrolling and looking for enemy combatants.

Our 'enemy' was in the shape of Gurkhas who had been brought in for the exercise and had built an enemy camp somewhere which we would have to find and assault. Those were some hard days, constantly forging our way through the thick primary jungle under heavy bergens in the oppressive heat and humidity, forever on edge in case we were 'bumped' by the enemy and had to go through our immediate action drills and contact drills, and I would collapse in my hammock or A-frame at night, too knackered to worry that much about the jungle cohabitants in the undergrowth around us.

I think most Special Forces guys would agree that the jungle is the most demanding part of selection. It combines all the key elements of good soldiering, fieldcraft, map reading, tactics, camouflage, admin and teamwork. If you have a weakness as a soldier, the jungle will find you out.

We concluded with a long exercise on 'hard routine', which meant no fires or lights, so that we had to eat our rations cold. We would wake up really early in the morning, about half an hour before it started to get light, and get out of our 'dry clothing' and put on our wet clothing, which we'd been wearing during the day for the last couple of weeks. We would then collapse our hammocks silently, put on fresh cam cream and clean our weapons in the dark, so that by the time it started to get light we were all spread out in fire positions facing outwards, silent and alert. After ten or fifteen minutes we would slowly get up in pairs, put on our packs and continue patrolling for an hour or so, then we would break track and peel back on ourselves to put an ambush on anyone who was following us. After lying there until we were sure we had not been followed, we would send the comms sched to base, telling them of our position, and then, in our pairs, have breakfast, which would be a cold foil wrap of corned beef hash, or if you were lucky, sausage and beans.

We would follow tracks, and every now and then would cross paths with the Gurkhas and trigger a firefight – using blanks, of course. At the end of the day, just before last light, we would get into all-round defence again and sit in fire positions facing outwards, and when it was finally dark we would get out our hammocks, assemble them in the dark and get our dry kit back on, making sure we had talc on our feet and our maps and compasses in our pockets. Our instructors would set up some way off from us and observe us from a distance, occasionally coming down to check if we all had items of kit on our person.

The exercise continued, now and then with one of the students asking to VW, and our numbers by the end of the exercise had shrunk. People grew tired and grouchy and claimed that they couldn't work as a team or didn't enjoy the jungle and its environment, or that they simply couldn't perform and found the soldiering and map work too difficult. By the time we'd concluded our exercise and were on the helicopter being extracted back out of the jungle, there were only twenty-six of us left.

When we returned to base camp we had a few days to clean up and scrub our kit ready to hand it back in. As the jungle phase progressed I had noticed how wild we were all looking, as we couldn't wash or shave and were not eating properly. Everyone had long shaggy beards and black faces, eyes popping out of their sockets, and most people had lost a lot of weight. I eventually saw it in myself when we got back to base and I visited the washroom. I hardly knew the man in the mirror!

We all shaved and washed and cleaned our kit, and though we were all pleased to have completed the jungle phase, we knew that some would be told they had not been up to the required standard and had to return to their units. It was going to be heart breaking for these guys who had given their all only to be told it wasn't enough. I just hoped it wouldn't be me. I did feel fairly confident, but there is always an element of doubt and we wouldn't be told until we returned to the UK, which seemed like an eternity away.

We flew back to the UK a few days later, and were given the rest of the weekend off without being told who had passed the jungle phase and who had not. It was an agonising wait for the Monday to come around, and it was all I could think about after having spent the last, and hardest, three months of my life battling to pass this course.

We all returned to Stirling Lines, and were told to wait in the cinema, where the training officer called out a number of names and told them to wait outside. It was approximately half of the guys, but which half had passed and which half had just fallen short?

When the training officer had finished his list he walked out of the cinema, where I was among the half who'd stayed put. The chief instructor then walked in and told those of us sitting in the room that we had passed.

I was overjoyed. It had all been worthwhile; halfway through the course and – as some might say – with the hardest part behind me, I was still there, although we were a seriously small group now.

The next phase was combat survival, when we were taught how to cope on our own in the elements and perhaps behind enemy lines. Combat survival is a tri-service course and the general army can do it. We are shown how to make improvised clothes and weapons, and set traps against humans and animals; learned what plants we could eat and which to avoid; and also shown how to collect water.

This seemed particularly topical after the exploits of the SAS in the Gulf War, when the problems the patrols faced were well documented in the books *Bravo Two Zero* and *The One That Got Away*, by ex-SAS guys Andy McNab and Chris Ryan.

We are then told that if we are captured, we can only tell the enemy the big four: name, rank, number and date of birth. I just tried to make myself small and insignificant. This would later become more relevant than I could have imagined.

We were then dressed in Second World War outfits, put on trucks that drove us out into the Welsh moors, and kicked out late at night, each with just a small sketch map and whatever survival kit we had managed to conceal on our person.

The map would give us a reference point which we had to reach several hours later to meet an 'agent' who was, in fact, one of the instructors. They would give us a very welcome cheese sandwich and our next RV (rendezvous point). At the same time, we had a 'hunter force' chasing us, which was another infantry unit equipped with helicopters, Land Rovers and sniffer dogs. They were given the rough area everyone was in and would just scour the countryside searching and trying to catch us. If we were caught, we were told, we would have to spend some hours 'in the bag', or under capture, where we would be put in stress positions and interrogated.

Going to ground in the barren countryside like a hunted animal, we tried to find cover, any kind of cover, wherever we could, and to remember all we'd been taught about combat survival. Keeping hydrated was the main thing, and also fed, if we could find anything growing wild to supplement the meagre food we were given. Remaining hidden whenever the hunter force got close was the other thing, and the strain of knowing they were getting nearer and nearer put us under enormous pressure.

The cat-and-mouse hunt went on for several days, and students feel themselves getting weaker and weaker as the days wore on and the hunter force got nearer and nearer. At least the nights were not as bitterly cold as they had been during our hills phase.

Whenever anyone got the opportunity to catch up with any of the other guys, they would normally take it, and they would try to stick together in small groups of three or four, drawing strength from each other, but if they were chased, they would split up and find themselves alone for days at a time until they met back up close to an agent RV.

Venturing out from the protection of the bracken where I had slept, I crept down to a largish stream one morning to refill my water bottle when I heard the noise of motorbikes nearby and the barking of dogs.

'Bollocks! The hunter force!' Had they tracked me or were they just searching blind?

I could probably make it to the edge of a nearby gully I had seen, where the motorbikes likely couldn't go, or I could crawl back into the thick bracken, but neither would hide me from the dogs that were bound to pick up on my scent.

The sound of voices and the barking grew closer, and I knew I had only a minute or less to make a decision, or else I would be caught like a rat in a trap and spend some time 'in the bag', as others had. It wasn't the dread of the stress positions that bothered me, but the sense of defeat that would fill me if I was caught.

I decided the stream was my only protection against discovery by the dogs and, spotting a couple of boulders midstream that were about the only thing that might hide me from sight, I scrambled across the riverbed and almost fully submerged myself in the pool of water that had been scoured out between the rocks.

I lay there, as still and as silent as I could, as the cold of the mountain water seeped into my bones and I shivered uncontrollably. I didn't know if the dogs could hear the pounding of my heart, but it sounded deafening to me, a bass drum thumping in my ears so that I couldn't hear if I was breathing loudly, my mouth barely clear of the water level.

It seemed like for ever, but eventually the sound of the dogs, and the roar of the motorbikes, faded into the distance.

I had got away with it.

At the end of the week we were all herded into a van and told we had finished and were being driven back to camp.

I had learned enough about this process not to believe the DS any time they told us we could relax, but it was hard not to give in to the soporific rocking of the van and the hypnotic drone of the rubber tyres on tarmac as we trundled along for a few hours.

We were all dishevelled and knackered, and while the warm air in the van lulled us into a snooze, it also intensified the putrid smell of our bodies, though not enough to bother me as I enjoyed this welcome respite from being hunted on the moors and began to give in to my exhaustion.

I was wrenched from my slumber as the van screeched to a halt, the back doors flew open, and armed guys in balaclavas surrounded us and forced us roughly out and onto the ground.

'Get out! Get out of the fucking van!'

'On your knees. Do it! Now!' they screamed.

Somewhere, shots were fired, and we were blindfolded then pushed and dragged into a compound. Failure to move fast enough earned a thump around the head or the back, and I was bundled into what seemed like a building, though I couldn't see.

The walls were solid enough as I was forced into a stress position and made to lean against one of them with my arms and legs spread.

A whack from what felt like a rifle butt on the inside of my legs told me my legs weren't far enough apart and that I was not in the amount of discomfort these people clearly meant me to be in.

'Keep your hands above your head', a voice shouted directly into my ear, and I could hear screaming.

'Who are you? What are you doing in our country?' another, foreign, voice yelled at me.

'Are you British military?'

'Maclachlan', I managed to blurt out, and my service number.

I knew that this was my capture and interrogation test, and I kept telling myself it wasn't real and that they couldn't really hurt me, but it certainly felt real, and someone seemed to have forgotten to tell the thugs pushing me around that they weren't meant to hurt us.

My muscles were screaming in discomfort at the unnatural position I had been placed in, and then the deafening sound started – a wall of droning, mind-numbing white noise and a cacophony of other jarring sounds was pounding from speakers.

Even above the noise I could hear shouting and screaming and people groaning, but I just kept myself focused and kept telling myself it had to end at some stage, and with a cup of tea rather than a bullet through the brain. There was no sign of any brew, however, but a swift dig to the kidneys was dealt out any time I dared to relax from the stress position that was making my muscles shake uncontrollably.

I don't know how long I was held like that before rough hands grabbed me again, forced my head down into my chest and frogmarched me out of the room and down what felt like a long narrow corridor, with a series of sharp left and right turns.

I was pushed into a room, forced down into a chair and then left in silence, my own mind torturing me as to what would happen to me next.

The lack of any noise was almost as unnerving as the white noise. Was I alone in the room? I felt like there was someone else in there with me, but no one spoke.

Then a shuffle of feet, my blindfold was ripped off and a powerful light switched on, dazzling my eyes before they had a chance to acclimatise.

'Who are you?' said a man I could just about make out on the other side of a desk, as my eyes got painfully used to the light.

I repeated my name, rank, service number and date of birth, but said I couldn't say anything more.

I waited for another thump from the gorillas who had removed my blindfold, but nothing came. They weren't there. Just the calm, reasonable bloke sat in front of me.

He asked again why I was there and what unit I was with, and again I apologised but said I couldn't tell him.

'You will tell us, or your friends will', he said, without a hint of anger in his voice, but with unmistakable menace.

Suddenly, the gorillas were behind me again. I was blindfolded, dragged out of the room and back down the corridor to the room of white noise.

I couldn't see, and even when I could there were no clocks, but by my estimates for about the next day I was forced, both in between and during questioning, into varying painful stress positions, from kneeling on the floor with my hands on my head to leaning against the wall with my hands outstretched, and always the deafening noise.

From time to time I would be dragged out, back down the corridor and into a different room.

I was subjected to around ten separate interrogations in all, anything from the good guy/bad guy routine; to being stripped naked and showered with a cold power hose and then ridiculed by a woman; to more mentally testing situations where the interrogators would try to trick you into writing or saying something.

As the hours went by I grew more tired, and it was hard to stay awake. I knew that this was another form of torture, and that sleep deprivation is a good way to make you confused and lose your alertness, but knowing it and being able to do anything to alleviate the exhaustion and disorientation are two different things.

Close to collapse, I was grabbed once more and hustled down the corridor, dreading whatever interrogation would be at the end of it this time, but when the blindfold was taken off, I registered that it was the chief instructor and medical officer in front of me.

'Hello, Maclachlan', said the instructor. 'Do you recognise me?' I did, but after hours of inquisition, and trying to stay alert to any pitfalls, it was hard to be sure.

He told me his name, which I knew. 'You see the white armband, don't you?' he said. 'I am the umpire, and this part of the phase is over. It's finished.'

It was difficult to accept that it was genuinely the end of the ordeal and not a trick, but I knew what he was saying had to be right.

I was examined by the doctor, then taken back through to an office and debriefed on my performance. It had gone well, and I had pretty much managed to keep track of time, which is quite hard to do in those circumstances.

I had passed the phase, but two more guys had failed, and our once huge cadre, which had filled the entire mess hall, was down to 6 per cent. I could have no idea just how much that training would have a bearing on my future Special Forces career.

The next phase involved parachuting, and again, because I'd never parachuted before, I was looking forward to it. There were a few Paras on the phase who, of course, had done all this, and they were sent on continuance training like languages or weapon training. I was a bit nervous at first because this was all new to me, but everyone on the course was in the same boat, so I just got on with it. By the end I quite enjoyed it and concentrated on being more accurate with my landings, as opposed to just being glad to be alive at the end of the jump.

The course was around a month long, with the odd weekend off, and we stayed on the RAF base at Brize Norton in Oxfordshire and all slept in old Second World War-style tin huts.

One night, after a particularly eventful evening, I was driving the rest of the lads back into camp when I was pulled over by a Military Police man who thought I was speeding and, due to the 20 miles per hour speed limit, there was every chance that he was right! I agreed and tried to appear amiable, but the rest of the guys in the car were all pissed and trying to have a laugh with him.

MPs are not known for their sense of humour, and as this one went to walk away, one of the lads tooted the horn, and he ran back across to warn me that if he heard the horn once more he would arrest me. I apologised and slowly drove off, but just as we rounded the corner the lads honked the horn, this time much longer and louder, and I could see him in the rear-view mirror running towards his car. I floored it and got airborne over every speed bump between there and the huts.

We all ran in and dived under our blankets just before we heard the screeching of tyres and the door fly open. He stood in the doorway shining his flashlight around, and I nearly creased up with laughter at the sight of all the pairs of shoes sticking out from under the covers. He stood there for a moment or two, then slammed the door back behind him to a chorus of laughter all round.

We completed the jumps course and spent the next two weeks on signals training. This was rather less exciting than the rest of the course, but just as important, as we had to learn to send secret messages over a variety of means of communication and study the use of different codes.

The next few weeks were much more exciting, with the next package, which was essentially the bread and butter of the SAS. We practised CQB, or close-quarters battle, in the 'killing house'. We practiced nearly every situation and eventuality until it was muscle memory and instinctive. Dressed in black Nomex flame-resistant suits and wearing respirators, we used shotguns and demolitions to enter the stronghold, and stun grenades and hand signals once inside. This was a lot of fun, and we practised many different methods of inserting into buildings, like helicopter onto the roof, or abseiling through windows. We practised on all modes of transport, and by the end of the four weeks the mechanics of storming a room in a team were second nature.

At the end of this phase, we were eventually badged. This was what we'd all been waiting for, and I was expecting some kind of big passing-out parade, but we were just met in the classroom by the CO, who gave us all our berets, said a quick, 'Well done', and left. And that was that.

We were then told to report to our squadrons.

It was over, I was now badged. From what seemed hundreds in the cookhouse only 6% finished! I had finally passed selection, and was sent to D Squadron, Mountain Troop.

On Saturday, 27 January 2024, the SAS troopers who had all passed selection with me did the Fan dance in allocated time to celebrate the twenty-fifth-year anniversary – and celebrate the fact we were all still alive. Just.

When I reflect on SAS selection, it occurs to me that sometimes we can be guilty of comparing and measuring ourselves to others. In reality though, there is no one else like us. That is what makes us unique. There were loads of people in the canteen, people that were far bigger, stronger and fitter than me and if I had tried to compare myself to them there is a chance I would have come up short, even if it was just in my own head. Sometimes, being just 'you' is enough. In my case, I felt like I was middle of the road and perfectly average compared to these guys, but average in a special group of people is fine. When there was just twelve of us at the end I was still just 'in the middle somewhere'. I would rather be ranked mediocre in an elite group of people than great in an average group of people. Remember that.

'I believe success is achieved by ordinary people with extraordinary determination.'

Zig Zigler

'WHO DARES WINS'

It was June 1999 and I had arrived. I had made it. I was a member of the elite: the renowned 22 Special Air Service Regiment. But if I had expected a trumpet fanfare as I walked through the gates of Stirling Lines as a newly badged trooper, I would have been sorely disappointed.

The iconic statue of Sir David Stirling, the founding father of the SAS, sat outside the HQ building, and just to see it there had my heart beating a little prouder in my chest.

At the other end of the camp was 'The Clock', the 30-feet tall, four-sided clock monument that carries the names of every SAS man killed while in service.

At the base is inscribed a verse from *The Golden Journey to Samarkand* by James Elroy Flecker, which sums up the intrepid spirit of the regiment and a yearning for faraway adventure.

> *'We are the Pilgrims, master; we shall go*
> *Always a little further...'*

I wanted to go further, across snow-covered mountains; across glimmering seas...

> *'... but surely we are brave,*
> *'Who take the Golden Road to Samarkand.'*

Only time would tell how brave I would be, but the names on the monument were a permanent reminder of the bravery of men who had gone before me.

There is a saying in the regiment that someone who retires after a life in the SAS 'has beaten the clock'. Little did I know at that stage how many of my contemporaries would not beat it, but would honour it with their names.

Just hearing that Flecker verse still brings a lump to my throat, but having walked through the new Stirling Lines gates that first time, I was reminded of the lack of fellow brave pilgrims I had noted from my previous time at the old base.

The camp is like most other military establishments. Building for each of the squadrons and headquarters and stores, and of course the famous clock tower. It can be bustling with guys at times but for the most part people are away doing exercises, courses or operations etc. Inside the buildings, a wealth of experience and history and memorabilia from wars and operations gone by.

The complete absence of hustle and bustle on my arrival was a million miles from the scenes of madness that had greeted me on my first day at the depot, and I was to find a very relaxed attitude around camp, with no fixed uniform, as such, and people with hands in pockets, long hair and no headdress; people on first-name terms with each other, with perhaps only the CO being called 'Boss'.

It was a far cry from those drill squares and sergeant majors of Werl, Fort George and Colchester, and the contrast suited me down to the ground, but fitting in would not be quite so simple.

The regiment is like most others where they go through 'cycles' of operations, exercises, promotional courses and standby for UK based stuff. I joined on 'the team' phase, which is probably the worst part of the cycle as you are just based in Hereford awaiting a call for anything. The best time is to go straight out onto an operation as then you have nothing to prove to anyone and you are accepted far quicker into a squadron. The team, as it implies, is basically when the squadron are on standby for an event similar to the Iranian Embassy siege in London Princes Gate, where the SAS were first revealed to the public via the news and TV sets in 1980.

In terms of exercises, the SAS were deployed to major Army Training Centres around the world to brush up on jungle, arctic or desert warfare. A lot of the courses were the same you would expect to do, although some were specialised. These weren't courses you personally chose. They were chosen for you. Every man needed a good working knowledge of all aspects of SAS skills, including weapons, languages, demolitions or medical, and although we were far from the green army, SAS soldiers still had to pass junior and senior command courses at the infantry training school. No one escapes the Brecon Beacons! After all the phases were complete, the squadron would then repeat the entire cycle, taking over on each transition from the squadron one step ahead in the cycle.

Crashing in on the team phase as a new bloke wasn't without its problems. It was seen as the worst time to join a squadron, on account of the fact that, during the counter-terrorism preparations, it takes far longer to be accepted. New guys received a lot of scrutiny during this phase from the more senior members of the squadron, which I could understand to a degree, but receiving stick from guys who had joined just one or two intakes before me seemed a bit much. I don't recall getting any advice, any welcome or any guidance, and it seemed that, instead of offering the slightest bit of help, people were happy to let you make mistakes before pointing out the error of your ways.

I crossed paths with a couple of individuals in particular who made sure that my first few months were fairly inhospitable.

It was ironic that several months prior to selection, and while on my recce commander's course in Warminster, I had been sitting in the sergeants' mess with my friend Cookie, who had previously attempted selection and hadn't passed the jungle phase. He had always wanted to join the SAS and was gutted to have failed, but he was even more disappointed to see that another guy on his selection course had passed. He pointed the guy out and said he was totally disillusioned with the whole selection process because, in his opinion, this guy was useless.

As fate would have it, the very same guy that Cookie described was in my squadron and, shock horror, he was finding fault with everyone – especially me. During a transport option, which was a set of different scenarios we practised involving a terrorist incidents on all modes of transport, I asked the guy for a small piece of his black electrical tape for my earpiece. My request was met by a torrent of criticism involving accusations of the misuse of electrical tape and assertions of how, as he was in charge of demolitions, he couldn't afford to dish out his tape willy-nilly. Open-mouth breathing for about twenty seconds to calm down, I then walked over to my kit for some of my own tape, only to watch one of the senior lads walk across and ask him for the same thing and, of course, be given the entire fucking roll without so much as a squeak.

Moving on, after a visit to the local DIY shop to stock up on tape, I found myself overseas to train a specialist sub unit, and this time, while I was unloading one of the shotguns, my 'electrical tape' friend came steaming across and started tearing a strip off me in public. He insisted that he had spotted with his eagle eye that I had pointed the weapon at one of the guys while I was unloading it.

Now, being from an infantry background, I prided myself on my weapon handling, and didn't appreciate the 'soldier's five' from an ex-signaller. Naïvely, I tried to point out that I had made no such mistake, but he closed me down with a condescending, 'If you want to ignore sound advice from a senior bloke then be it on your head…'

He left, but not before I was reminded of his accumulated service of twelve years in the Royal Signals. I bit my tongue and busied myself, and just two days later, like a ray of sunshine, karma came round in the shape of a negligent discharge by my supercilious 'senior' colleague. He fired a weapon off by mistake just inches from a colleague's face. Luckily, the ammunition was blank, so the damage was minimal. It was to happen again a few years later when we found ourselves on the same sniper course, and once more he had a negligent discharge, this time with a sniper rifle. Thankfully, he wasn't that great a shot, and needless to say, I didn't hear too much from him after that.

For those first months, though, the days were long, and I found it hard to settle. I loved learning new skills, but the politics of the work environment were alien to me. I realised that a game was being played, and that in order to take the heat off themselves, there were people who'd find any pretext they could to criticise others.

I stuck with the friends that I'd made on selection. We had passed together, and invariably we would work together in the future. As the heat increased that late summer, we spent a fair amount of time on the ranges, and like most soldiers, tops were removed and operational bronzing commenced, only to find that we were bollocked for it and given shite duties for the remainder of the cycle.

A few weeks later, a couple of lads were shooting rabbits and birds at the range, so I decided to join in, and was instantly reprimanded for my efforts. I felt like a heat seeker and began to wonder why I had bothered putting myself through so much in order to wear the beret if I was going to be treated like this. To use the word bullying would be over the top, but I'd been through some of that as a child, so the last thing I expected was to have to suffer similar thoughts during the early stages of being an SAS trooper. I understood that you start at the bottom and build up, but I felt like the new blokes were being torn down before they had started. So what was selection for?

Four months into that phase, my task of the day was to sweep the hangar where we were based. It contained our lockers and vehicles and had an armoury for our weapons. Mundane as they were, I understood that these tasks were an absolute must. The SAS above sweeping a hangar? No chance. When I had finished I looked about to see what was happening, and I found that everyone else had left, so I walked out to where our offices were to see if there were any notes for detail tomorrow. Looking at the whiteboard, I saw a message, 'Wed PT/CQB.' With no one about, I went into the SSM's (Squadron Sergeant Major) office to ask what it meant, as there were no timings, locations or instructions on what kit was required. He seemed bemused but went through, in detail, the proposed events for the following day. I apologised for having interrupted him and said that I'd been cleaning the hangar and hadn't been told. He said that people in the SAS were grown-ups and, unlike the green army, didn't need telling what to do every five minutes. I agreed to a point, but just couldn't get my head around nobody talking to one another. It was like you had to be in the right room or company to know what the fuck was going on.

Passing selection didn't magically allow me to suddenly see further than my own nose, but in my old regiment, if a new guy turned up, someone would look out for him, help him dodge the potholes, and that was the one thing I missed from the green army. You are never so good that you don't need the occasional quick word on a task or a weapon system. I told the SSM I wanted posted back to the Royal Scots, he was gobsmacked and reminded me that I hadn't done all that hard work the last six months to pass selection to give up after four months of being here, but I was completely disillusioned with 'SAS life'. I knew I would enjoy it more back in my old unit, where perhaps the job wasn't exactly the same but the atmosphere and camaraderie was far higher. He said he would sort a meeting with the boss, but the next day the OC asked me to experience at least two years there so I could have a far rounder experience, and I reluctantly agreed. The rest, as they say, is history.

*'When everything seems to be going against you,
remember that the airplane takes off against
the wind, not with it.'*

Henry Ford

A SPECIAL FORCES OPERATOR

Towards the end of my time on the team I was on an FAC (Forward Air Controller) course when it came over the news about a hijacked jet coming into Stansted. It was February 2000 and the events of the hijacked jet and what followed are well documented. The plane had been on an internal flight within Afghanistan from Kabul to Maser-e-Sharif on Sunday, 6 February with 186 passengers and crew on board when it was hijacked. After initial stops in Uzbekistan and Kazakhstan, the plane landed in Moscow where it refuelled and then set course for the UK. The plane landed at Stansted at around 2.00 am on Monday, 7 February. Contingency plans were activated, and Essex Police took control initially on the ground. Eight hostages were released on the Monday and another left on Tuesday. The pilot and crew members also escaped from the cockpit on Tuesday. On Wednesday, a crew member was thrown through the door with minor injuries. From around 3.30 am onwards the remainder of the plane were slowly released from the plane resulting in a successful negotiation and all hostages rescued safely.

During my time off I decided to buy a house in Hereford. I didn't have much money, but I'd saved enough to put down a deposit and have some left over for some basic furniture. The rest of the niceties could wait as I could buy a new piece each month. It was a good move, and luckily the house was not too far from the camp. My home helped me to feel like I was getting away from the work environment, and it was a place I could relax. Moving into our 'exercise' phase, we were due to go to Africa on a bush-type exercise. In the regiment you are issued with a lot of kit, and the clothing and equipment is matched to all the different environments you might face. We always had a number of backpacks and bags pre-packed that were suitable for desert, arctic or jungle operations, so that we could move with minimum notice to anywhere in the world. I used to have a cage in the block at Stirling Lines where I would keep all my bags and equipment, and I would just drive in and out of the camp every day, unencumbered by different bergens. Exercises were always hard work, as we would train for real, and we would usually go out to another country and have a range package. This would ensure that all our weapons were working and serviceable in that particular climate and that each one of us could acclimatise quickly. Without any major incidents while we were in our 'standby' phase, the squadron moved into the 'promotions' phase, and I was sent on my Mountain Leader's course. My friend Dekka, who I had passed selection with, was on the same course, which made it all the more enjoyable.

The first part of the course was in Hereford and around the local area, and it took us all through basic climbing techniques. There were some other lads on the course who had been in the regiment a year or two before me, and they were good guys, great to get on with and keen to share their knowledge and help me along. Once we knew our carabiners from our crampons and our up from our down, we went to Switzerland and had a go at some harder climbs and also some ice climbing. We went into the hills and learned about the weather, avalanches, leading routes, altitude and rescue, and we even did some skiing. When we returned to the UK we were sent to Wales, where we practised everything we'd learned – apart from the skiing – and were given our qualifications. It was almost like a holiday, and we were being paid to learn how to climb and ski! I wasn't that comfortable with heights and I wasn't great at climbing, but luckily Dekka, who was far bigger and stronger than me, would usually climb up first then pull me up after him!

With my Mountain Leader credentials secured, I was sent on my Medics course. That might conjure up visions of simple battlefield first aid, but the SAS doesn't do things by halves. The course consisted of six weeks in a classroom studying anatomy and practising basic techniques, and then we were sent to hospitals around the UK for four-week placements, working in and around all the departments, including A&E. After this we went on a trauma refresher where all the top consultants from around the UK came in and briefed us on revised techniques, whereupon we received our qualifications. The first six weeks were fascinating, and I enjoyed learning something useful and potentially lifesaving. We practised everything from putting in lines to suturing, chest drains and even crikes (cricothyrotomy) which is an emergency procedure for cutting into someone's blocked airway to allow them to breath.

The next four weeks were just as good, as I was sent to an A&E department to experience real-life trauma treatments with all the staff. I went with John, another guy from the squadron, and we had a really good time. From the very first day we were thrown in at the deep end and called upon to put chest drains on both sides of a patient who had fallen while painting a flagpole. It was daunting at the time but gratifying that the staff had a lot of faith in our ability and, after watching us in action, put their trust in us, allowing us to practise many different procedures under their supervision. About a week into our attachment, we were enjoying lunch at a trendy bar and got chatting to a friendly young waitress from Australia. After finishing our lunch, we returned to the A&E department to find we were being sent to spend the afternoon with the hospital's quick response ambulance fitted out and able to react to any situation within the town centre at a moment's notice.

No sooner had we been given the brief about all the fittings and equipment and their normal operating procedures than a shout came from the Tannoy and we were off. We found that we were going to the bar we had just come from – some masonry had fallen from the roof and caused some severe casualties. The scene was a shambles, and the dust was still settling from the concrete and rubble. We couldn't help but notice that the masonry had impacted right around the outside table at which we had been sitting just half an hour before.

Several people were lying on the ground, and these were the first that we went to. I tried to remember everything I had been taught, looking for massive bleeds first, and then airway problems. There was a woman lying unconscious on the ground with a pool of blood around her head, and I went straight to her. As I worked on trying to stabilise her, I saw that it was the young Australian waitress from lunch. I couldn't believe it. We'd been chatting such a short time before, and now here she was in a bad way, with blood flowing from a basal skull fracture. We rushed her back in the ambulance, and everyone did their utmost to save her, but sadly she died. It would have been upsetting enough to lose any patient, but this was particularly gut-wrenching, as we'd got along so well with this young girl less than an hour previously and had picked up on her zest for life and her enthusiasm at being on an adventure so far from home. Another shock came the next day when the incident, and the accident scene, was splashed all over the front page of the local newspaper. We were supposed to be maintaining a low profile, and we'd told everyone we were just army paramedics, but there we were, involved in front-page news.

Still a little jumpy at this unexpected exposure, I was alarmed a few days later when we heard a request over the speaker system asking for the 'two guys who had just arrived from the SAS' to report to reception. John was furious and stormed off to reception, where he gave them a bollocking for telling the whole hospital that we were SAS. The woman behind the desk looked bemused for a moment, and then laughed and told him not to get too excited, as she'd only been requesting the two drivers with the Ambulance Service to check in! I couldn't stop laughing for ages, much to John's embarrassment.

But his own turn to laugh came around a week later, when a nice-looking nurse on attachment from New Zealand, who was working in the ward we were on at the time, came across and asked if we could suture. I jumped at the chance to impress her and said there wasn't much I didn't know about suturing. With that she brought a young man over who had slit his eyelid almost all the way across, and I was stunned. I was used to simple cuts on the arms or back and had never touched anyone's face before. This sort of thing was usually left to plastic surgeons.

I couldn't back down now that I was committed, and I asked for the needle and thread. John loved every minute of this and was hovering over my shoulder as I began. My hands were shaky at the best of times, and this was no place to get nervous. The nurse was supervising my first few stitches and she said that we obviously had a different technique in the army, and she hadn't seen my method before! I stammered back that this was the best method to use and ensured a good tight join but might leave a slightly bigger scar. She reluctantly agreed and watched as I quickly finished off.

I thought I'd come out of it scot-free until two days later, when John spotted the man coming back through the front door with his eyelid stuck to his eyebrow, saying he wanted to complain, as he hadn't slept for two days. John and I decided to go for an early lunch break.

I like to think we pulled our weight in giving decent medical care to the patients, but there were some funny incidents as well, and one day I was asked to assist in a case where a man had put an entire biro pen down his penis. While the nurses held him in place, I eased out the offending article with forceps and then returned to my desk in a state of shock. I was told he'd been 'experimenting' when this happened, and it was all I could do not to burst out laughing at the description. A short while later the man appeared from the treatment bay limping and looking decidedly sheepish. He must have thought I was the doctor and asked me if he was required to sign anything, and I found myself saying, 'Why? Do you want your pen back?' The whole ward erupted into giggles, and I felt sorry for the guy as he limped out of the hospital, but I thought to myself that now I'd seen it all.

We had a great time touring the hospitals, and I was surprised by just how much responsibility John and I were given. There were medical students who had completed almost five years of a medical degree who were not even allowed into the resuscitation rooms, and there we were putting in lines and chest drains, conducting CPR and just roaming freely around the wards taking bloods, examining X-rays, applying plaster casts and writing reports.

We returned at the end of our time in A&E and were sent to Austria and then Norway as part of our Nordic training. Here we practised skiing and ice climbing and living in snow holes. This had more of a military approach, and we had our full array of weapons and packs while we patrolled and went about the exercise.

During the final exercise I was flying downhill in my usual harum-scarum style, due to the heavy pack and Minimi machine gun hanging around my neck, when one of my skis got caught in a branch sticking out from the ground and I did a most ungraceful forward somersault, ripping all my shoulder ligaments in the process.

I tried to carry on, but it was too painful, and an MRI scan showed that I'd split my rotator cuff and would need to return to the UK for treatment. I was gutted to go back on my own without the squadron, but there was no alternative, so I returned to Hereford for some much-needed physio.

During this time, I managed to get on a colloquial Spanish language course, which I enjoyed, although it was cut short because I was due to go back out with the squadron to Belize on a jungle exercise. It was my first time in Belize, and my first time in the jungle since being in

East Africa. Compared with the jungle work we did on selection, it was a lot more chilled out, and we were not under direct scrutiny this time.

We went through all the similar jungle-type lessons that we'd undergone on selection, and then we went on different week-long packages like ranges, patrols and attacks that culminated in a final assault. It was hard going but enjoyable, and we learned how to set up ambushes and fire all sorts of weapon systems.

When we returned to the main camp after the exercise, and had finished cleaning and packing, we were released to go downtown, although there weren't that many places to go. One notorious haunt used by all the troops on exercise in Belize was a club called Raul's Rose Garden. It was just a strip bar and knocking-shop selling cheap beer, but there was trouble there that night, and I noticed one local-looking lad arguing with some of the Gurkhas who were posted to Belize and who often played the role of the enemy in exercises.

The next day, we were told that the prime minister's 17-year-old son had been killed there the night before. In fact, although he had been one of four wealthy local teenagers attacked, it was the 14-year-old son of a local millionaire fruit tycoon who had died. It was a serious incident, and even when we returned to the UK the Special Investigation Branch (SIB) continued to take statements from everyone who had been there. I was a pretty good witness, as I was one of the few who could remember anything, having not drunk any alcohol that night. As it turned out, a group of Gurkhas had beaten the 14-year-old so badly that he had died.

The jungle in Belize is considerably dirtier than in Borneo, in the sense that you can catch more tropical diseases and stuff in Belize – and not just from Raul's Rose Garden. This became evident about a month after we returned, when guys started to develop sores, which eventually turned out to be leishmaniasis, a skin-eating disease that develops from sandfly bites. More and more people went down with it, and I was one of the last. It started as a small sore on my hand and gradually got worse and worse until it was an open seeping sore. I was sent to Aldershot along with a couple of other lads, and we had to spend over three weeks getting treatment there. It was an ordeal. We had to take jabs every day with a solution which, in a more undiluted strain, was used as a poison for cattle. After around a week I couldn't move or eat, and all my joints ached. It took me ages to recover, and I could hardly run the length of myself when I got out. My running and cardiovascular fitness was never the same again and even months later, I could hardly catch my breath trying to run for any duration.

When I did recover I was sent to Brecon on a machine-gun course, mainly so that I could run a gun line back in the regiment, but also so that I could judge whether it would be worthwhile to send blokes on these courses in future.

I turned up relatively unprepared, and when they gave me an initial assessment, I realised that I knew nothing. The rest of the guys came from the machine-gun platoons in their various battalions and were all over it. Nevertheless, I enjoyed the first week. Although it was mainly revision for the rest of the guys, it was all new to me, and I learned a lot.

After that, though, the course became more and more laborious. We would spend a whole week on attack, then another on defence and then one on patrols, and it could have been done at shorter intervals. The regiment was running its own mortar course at the same time, and in three weeks the lads had covered three different types of mortar, including live firing, and had done all the range quals. My course was six weeks and covered just one machine gun!

Inevitably, I grew frustrated on more than one occasion. There was one time, on the defence package, when we spent all night trying to dig a trench into the side of a quarry and then were just told to watch the area to our front, or our 'killing ground'… for a whole week. It did nothing but rain the whole time, and after a couple of days we watched in disbelief as the officers conducted a lesson of their own, on our supposed 'killing area'. We were visited just once a day for around ten minutes to check that we weren't all asleep, and that was it.

After around four days I'd had enough and left to go and find the DS to ask why nothing was happening. I couldn't find anyone, and later discovered that it was because they were going home every day! At the end of the week our DS came along and fired off a burst from his rifle, telling us we were being 'bugged out'. We then hurriedly left our shell scrapes and made our way back to our safe haven, which was the waiting trucks.

I didn't understand the logic behind this pointless exercise, and when we arrived back at base, I went straight in to see the OC to ask what had been achieved. He said that it had all been part of the course to see how we would cope in the muddy conditions. I told him I thought it had been a complete waste of a week. We hadn't managed to fire our weapons, and we hadn't even been monitored while we were there, so how did they know how we were coping?

About half an hour later I rubbed all the staff up the wrong way even more; the DS asked me to empty their truck, which contained fridges, heaters, rations and cot beds. I was furious and refused and told the OC afterwards. We had spent all week in the field, and I had all my muddied kit to clean, while these guys had been staying nice and dry in warm accommodation with heaters and hot food, and we were expected to clean and tidy their stuff up as well!

Some of the ranges were quite good, and we were given a lot of ammunition, but some were poor. At one point we had travelled all night to form up in a line on the side of a hill overlooking another forward-facing slope, which was our range, but because it was 6.00 am and the ranges were not officially open until 9.00 am, we were told to wait. We were then told that one guy from each pair could go up and collect 3,000 rounds of ammunition.

I immediately got up with my partner and went to collect it, and that caused the DS to bawl me out for coming up the hill, as he'd asked for only one guy. I explained to him that 3,000 rounds was a lot of ammunition, and I knew how heavy that was and how difficult it would be to carry it.

Sure enough, the rest of the lads were struggling, and one of them even broke the straps of his bergen trying to carry it all. The DS pulled me to one side and said the whole point of the exercise was to show how heavy the ammunition was and the effort involved, but I told him that no one in a real situation would just sit back on the gun line knowing his mate couldn't carry the ammo and that they couldn't operate the gun without it.

There was another instance on the course when we marched all night and finally got to a small ridge, where we set up the gun line and at first light fired down onto a simulated enemy position. After we'd marched back to base, we were told to get back onto the trucks, and we found ourselves being driven back out to the area to clean up. There was no one with us and one of the trucks nearly slid off the road. When we eventually reached what we thought was the location, we all got off and fanned out looking for the area, but there was no DS with us and none of the Gurkha drivers knew where we were either.

Suddenly, everyone was shouting – one of the guys had fallen into a large hole. It was then that I discovered we were in an impact area for artillery, so we all left and headed back to base, whereupon I asked the OC why we had no DS there to guide us and no medic cover. He said they should have been with us and also that there were range huts all over the training area, but I reminded him that they were not open until 7.00 am.

I'm sure they were glad when I finally left; I told them I wouldn't recommend the course to the regiment, because what had taken six long weeks could have been condensed into two, one of instruction and revision, and one of live firing, and they all agreed.

There were other courses that I attended where, rather than just shut up and do what the instructors said without question, I would query it or argue some other point, and this was out of step with military doctrine. Well, we were Special Forces and supposed to be 'thinking soldiers'.

The BG or bodyguard course, however, didn't give me much to complain about. There we were taught everything from personal protection of a client to working as a team, driving and writing risk assessments.

I'd been taken off the previous course to make room for my troop commander, an officer who was to spend just two years at the regiment and then return to his old unit having not used his trade once. I was disappointed, as this seemed like a great course to be on, with most of my close friends, Dekka and Dave – both of whom lived with me for a short time in Hereford – and Jim, Neil and Luke, some other really good lads from the squadron, who went to some fine places for training all across Europe.

I had to wait for a later course and settle for a single trip to Bristol, as I think they'd blown the entire budget on the previous course! Not long after this, some soldiers were taken hostage in Sierra Leone and again it was about being in the right place at the right time. It was September 2000 and civil war had been rumbling away in Sierra Leone and the RUF (Revolutionary United Front) were embroiled in an armed conflict with the government. In May that year, Britain had deployed troops there to evacuate foreign citizens and support a UN peacekeeping force.

On 25 August 2000, a vehicle patrol with eleven soldiers from the Royal Irish Regiment were surrounded and taken hostage.

After a few years, around 2002, I was sent on a Special Forces Commander's course, which showed me how to write reports, fill in request forms and complete soldiers' CRs (Confidential Reports). The course showed us the different departments of the regiment and how it all worked, and even had a table-top exercise in which we all role-played the different key personalities of the regiment in an operational situation. A lot of that was some way beyond a senior corporal's pay grade, but I completed it nevertheless, and by the time I returned to the squadron it was time to go on exercise again.

The unit were going back out to the desert on a mobility exercise and had just been given another new vehicle to trial in the desert. We were sent on special driving and mechanics courses in order to learn how best to handle this beast and how to carry out basic fault finding on the vehicle, and then we were sent to the coast, to practise on the sand before being really tested in the hot, harsh climates of Jordan.

The exercise in the desert started with us practising navigation, which we were all well versed in by now from the last two years in the 'pinkies'. These famous old vehicles had been signature jeeps for the SAS from the deserts of the Second World War and have been modified in various ways since they were first brought in. Many people recognise these, and they were brought to life in recent TV and film such as *SAS: Rogue Heroes* or *Ministry of Ungentlemanly Warfare*. There was a feeling of déjà vu, and everyone was probably sick of the sight of the desert and covering the same ground. We went back to the usual daily rigmarole of putting up cam nets and poles over the vehicles during the day and driving at night, and many thought the unit had lost a sense of realism after their live exploits in Iraq during the 1990 war.

The final exercise was going to be an advance on foot several kilometres up a wadi (ravine) and onto a high feature where the fire-support position would be set up. The rest of the team would then peel around the edge of the feature and fan out into an attack formation, covering each other while we assaulted various mocked-up bunkers.

Our Troop and Boat Troop were the first to find the 'enemy camp', and we spent the first three nights exploring the area and the enemy position, finding the best route to it and the best way to attack it, based on the locations of the bunkers. When rest of the squadron turned up, I and one other built a 3D model, simply made out of basic materials, to show the rest of the lads the layout of the camp and the scale.

When orders had finished, I was told to report to Nick, the SQMS, and I was surprised when he told us to take the SF (Sustained Fire) kit with us on the assault. These were essentially machine guns, but were intended for ranges of over 800 metres, and I asked why we were taking them, as I knew there were no positions more than 800 metres away.

Nick was furious with me for even questioning him and told me it was unprofessional behaviour for a senior corporal. He told me we were playing the exercise for real and that the troop commander, who hadn't even been in the regiment a year, had told him that there were positions a kilometre away. I couldn't believe it. It seemed to me that as a corporal who not only had experience and was trained in SF, but had been on the recce of the enemy camp the previous three nights in a row, I could expect my word to count for more than that of a newly joined officer.

But maybe this was being done to prove a point to somebody, so I carried the SF kit and got on with it.

The internal politics, the principle of not knowing why you are doing something but just doing it because you are told to – or because that's how the particular head shed (person(s) in charge) likes doing it – this was not something I was used to, and I had come to the regiment to avoid it.

But I wasn't alone in feeling disillusioned. As is often the case, post-conflict, many guys thought they had seen the best of things and were unlikely to replicate it in the near future.

I tried to look further ahead in the hope of brighter times and a change of scenery. After all, I was long overdue a posting, and had spent over six years in the squadron, completing three cycles, when most guys were posted after four or five years. I was looking forward to a change and had requested a posting to another unit, such as the Internal Capability Cell and the OC had agreed that there were several suitable postings for me.

I clung on to this as my escape from the squadron, and because the head shed at the time were starting to make a name for themselves, with the SSM and SQMS caustically known among the troopers as Uday and Qusay, after the two degenerate sons of Saddam Hussein.

A few guys who decided to quit and signed off (i.e. had paid to leave the army) were immediately blacklisted and kicked out of the squadron. The SSM got us all together and gave us a brief to the effect that if anyone didn't want to be part of the squadron then he didn't want them in it. Then he sent the three guys who had signed off to HQ squadron. But on the following Monday morning the three guys reappeared, after it came to light that the SSM couldn't expel them from the squadron simply for signing off.

Those were uneasy times in the squadron, and life turned bleak for a while, as we kept getting briefs in the mornings that were more like petty rants than professional information. Everyone came to expect morning talks that would leave us feeling like naughty juveniles, with lives dictated by rules and regulations.

But salvation was at hand. Fairly soon we learned that we would be returning to the Overseas, and the teams and patrols were put on the noticeboard. The British Army was deployed in both Iraq and Afghanistan at the time. I was sent with the rest of the squadron to the Middle East in a command position. I had just been made up to sergeant, and I guess this was the reward for my new seniority.

The posting delighted me, as this was something different. I noticed, however, that there were only two other guys with me, and that these two were straight off the last selection, brand new to the squadron.

This seemed strange, as normally in these circumstances it was the more senior guys who went on 'team tasks', and it was a common joke that you couldn't get on a team task until you had been on a team task, which didn't make any sense, and it was always the older guys and squadron favourites who were picked for these jobs.

I went to speak to the two guys, Lee and Seamus, and was horrified to find out that Seamus didn't have a driving licence, so I went to speak to the SSM and the OC but was told that there was nothing to be done, and he would be replaced once things had settled. This was a problem, but one I could do nothing to solve. I would just have to run with it.

With the new deployment on the horizon, all the lads practised in the assault teams to which they had been 'orbatted' (i.e. positioned into which teams etc.). I tried to practise in our small team but was told that the other teams were more important, so we were all split up and divided into the other teams to train with them.

I went up to Regimental HQ and asked for a sitrep from the team that was in place in the city my team and I would be going to, asking for the size of their team, routine, equipment, weapons and what they'd been up to in general, but it wasn't forthcoming. I kept going back to enquire until the guys there were sick of the sight of me, but I received no reply.

This was starting to worry me, as we were close to the date of departure and I still had no briefing on the task, so I went up to the ops cell and asked to phone the guys we were replacing so that I could ask them directly. When I told them why I wanted to phone I found that I couldn't: they were taking emergency calls only. Sometimes that's the fast-moving and fluid pace of operations, so I cracked on.

My only other hope was to visit the guys myself on the recce that the squadron would be sending out, but I found it would only be head shed going, so I asked for them to send me some info back. When the flight plans came out, I was hoping I might be on the advance party, but that didn't happen. Sometimes you just roll with the punches, so I hoped to make it work once in the theatre.

There's a case for being flexible when necessary, but in general I believe in sorting out the minor, seemingly lower-priority details as early as possible, as it means less risk when the main event begins. That belief would be hugely vindicated over the coming months and would lead me to a crossroads in my Special Forces career and ultimately lead to me making one of the most difficult decisions I've ever had to make – to leave the military altogether.

After complaining about the vehicles, equipment and SOPs we were assigned to, and being involved in a high profile incident overseas, which made me rethink my options.

I'm not permitted to talk about the details of the operation surrounding the incident, but when I left the service, I was granted EPAW (express prior authority in writing) to state I had been captured and had had treatment. I am now part of Hostage UK, an organisation that has some very interesting and inspiring characters and I am often asked to go and talk about what sort of things a hostage thinks about during capture, or life post-capture. Police academies, military training establishments and Foreign Commonwealth Offices primarily.

Whenever I think now about what a hostage goes through, or people that have been tortured or held for any period of time, it's a lonely, isolated world both during the event and thereafter. Your own mind is all you have for company and that can be your biggest friend or your worst enemy and that is all within that person's control. Nobody controls your emotions, only you, and that should give us strength. When people say 'he/that made me mad' – well actually that's impossible, we are the only gatekeepers to our emotions and although emotions are powerful, just armed with that fact can help us through some difficult times.

I moved to a different part of the country and was fortunate enough to be involved in an exchange programme with our US counterparts, which was great fun. Back in those days many people will be familiar with the infamous 'playing cards', a set of cards which had different foreign officials and high value government officials represented on them. I had a great time going after the playing cards, sometimes successfully and sometimes not. I was there for six months and still have many great US brothers in arms I still speak to today. On return back home, I volunteered to leave the SAS by 2006.

My last few months were not my happiest times, but the last few months of a career never are. I was due to be sent on troop training to Banff, Canada, as a final farewell, and went with Grant, our new troop staff sergeant down to the stores to sign out all the equipment and split it up between us. I was one of the most senior blokes going and would be giving a lot of the lessons to the other guys, so I was looking forward to it, but there were people determined that I should not bow out on a high. Although they knew they couldn't just kick me out of the squadron, I was given jobs like painting the office, hanging pictures and stacking shelves in the store.

The day before we were due to depart for Canada, I was called into the office by Nick, the new SSM, to be told that he and Grant didn't want me to go to Banff and that I was to report to the stores daily until I left the regiment. I was gutted. When I saw Grant he told me that it was Nick, and not him, who didn't want me to go, but it no longer mattered to me. They could do what they wanted. I told the CO as much when I left, and he advised me to consider a sabbatical. He said a regular posting was only two years, and if I took that slight sidestep many people would not even know that I'd left, in which time certain personalities, i.e. the SSM and SQMS (sergeant quartermaster sergeant) would have moved on.

I thanked him, but my mind was made up. I left, signing his guestbook, and handed my ID card in on the way out. I'd had my time and enjoyed it massively. I couldn't have joined at a better time for getting operational experience, and I had made a lot of friends for life, but I would never return. By the time I left the military in 2006, I had operated in every major operational theatre over the past two decades. The most difficult place I ever served was in the barracks. I wasn't a barracks soldier; I was a field soldier and best when I was out on operations and exercise. Fortunately, I didn't have to spend too long in the barracks at Hereford.

There is always a question about how much you can tell your friends and family about being in Special Forces. I think a blank denial to your wife can be quite hard when you're relocating to Hereford, being away for periods of six months and coming back with a tan, but a degree of commonsense probably applies. It's not for public consumption down the pub, but your pals in your old regiment would know because you went away on selection and never came back so it's not rocket science!

There have been a few books on life in the SAS but after the books by Andy McNab and Chris Ryan, the MOD made every candidate sign the disclosure document prohibiting anyone from writing anything regarding operations and having to go through the disclosure cell to receive EPAW for any manuscript relating to SF material. I had to go through this process, and this is why you rarely see any SF related material post-1991 in books. What I am permitted to say is that at that time the British Army was involved in places like Balkans, Northern Ireland, Sierra Leone, Iraq and Afghanistan.

That decade from 2000 to 2010 was a particularly busy period for our military and our SAS, and perhaps the busiest it has been since the Second World War. I am proud to have been part of it and been part of a group of men who were involved in some of the highest profile operations of the post-war era. The period following the Twin Towers attack would profoundly change the way the military worked and I was fortunate enough to do an exchange with other English speaking military forces as well as with the intelligence services.

The regiment is similar in many ways to others in that it is personality driven and one can simply join at a bad time or have particularly challenging head shed in charge at that time. I experienced this and left, like a vast cohort of my peers at that time, and it left a huge deficit in those with similar experience to me. The Commanding Officer at the time, Colonel Carleton-Smith, said I could leave for two years and then just re-enlist once the head shed had turned around and people would just think I was on a posting! This was unheard of at the time, guys being allowed to leave and just re-join, but we were haemorrhaging guys by the week and he had always been a horizon scanner. It was no surprise that he would later become Director of Special Forces and eventually in charge of the entire army.

I sometimes wonder what would have become of my life had I chosen that option, but we can never be stuck in the past, only just use it as a rudder to guide our future path – and mine was about to take a different route.

It was probably the bravest decision I ever made leaving the military. It was the only thing I knew from being a 16-year-old boy and I had reached the tip of the spear. Perhaps one of the top few hundred soldiers in the UK, if not the world, and here I was about to leave it all behind because of people and circumstances, for what? I didn't know I had a career on the other side, but I knew that, just like in my Special Forces career, I couldn't stand still. I had made a career from learning new skills, embracing things I didn't know I could do and thriving in that environment. I have friends now that come up to me and say 'I wish I had given it a go', and that must be a sad place to be as you can't go back and change history. If you are faced with these types of dilemmas of 'should I, shouldn't I?' and you are perhaps scared of failure or not being good at something, then face the fear and take it head on. I can assure you that the feeling of knowing (whether you succeed or not) is better than the feeling of never knowing. You win or you learn, in this case Who Dares *always* Wins!

'No one can tell what goes on in between the person you were and the person you become. No one can chart that blue and lonely section of hell. There are no maps of the change. You just come out the other side. Or you don't.'

Stephen King, *The Stand*

ALWAYS A LITTLE FURTHER

I've been asked a few times to compare the different Special Forces units. 'What's the best unit in the world'? is often a question or 'who is better, SAS or SBS', 'Is the SAS better than Delta Force or Seal Team 6?' Well, I'm probably biased, but it's worth mentioning that I can speak from some form of perspective, having served with them all. Just as few people on the planet have been involved in hostage negotiation, hostage rescue and been a hostage themselves, far fewer people have also served with the SAS, SBS, International Special Forces units, Secret Services and Governmental Security and Intelligence Services. Indeed, I wouldn't be surprised if I'm the only one. I'd spent some time with our various US counterparts between 2003 and 2006 and had been involved on an operational basis, as well as duties in security and intelligence.

I would say that every unit has its strengths and weaknesses and slightly different roles. In the SAS we recruit military-wide from the army, navy, RAF and Reserves – both men and women (albeit no woman has passed to date). We also have Ghurkas, Fijians, Australians, Kiwis, South Africans and many other nationalities, which gives us a very rich flavour of operators within our ranks. Our selection process is the hardest military test in the world. Fact. We know that from success rates which, it should be noted, recruit from a far higher gene pool in terms of soldiering skills. Our infantry units like the Paras and Marines are probably equivalent to some countries' Special Forces, and I include the Americans in that statement. I would pit our paratroopers against the US Rangers any day. Moreover, I would pit our paratroopers against any other infantry unit in the world (and quite a few countries' Special Forces).

In the SAS, your training never stops. The continuation training lasts a couple of years and then there are always new courses and skills you need to do, ranging from surveillance to weapons to languages to demolitions to medicine to management. We also cross train and skill other units in other countries so we are quite finely positioned to commentate on what units are 'better' than others. I would say that following on from 9/11 the US Special Forces were rightfully thrown a huge budget to go and get the job done, and some of their weapons, vehicles, predators, drones, NVGs (night vision goggles) and technical equipment are second to none – and something we could only dream of at Hereford. In terms of budgets, weapon systems, vehicles etc. the US is some way ahead in my opinion. That said, I always consider 'the operator' as the gauge of what is 'better' in terms of measurement, and there are few better than SAS operators for working on their own or in teams to get the job done.

There are always a lot of myths and rumours about the SAS. The size of guys, what they are capable of, martial arts, making themselves invisible and all sorts of nonsense, but people tend to forget we are just ordinary human beings. We have just had a different path in life. Ordinary people that have perhaps had extraordinary training and placed in extraordinary situations. You wouldn't give me or the other eleven guys that had passed selection a second glance in the street. We have to blend in to different environments and not stand out or look out of place. One thing that perhaps sets us apart from others is our resilience, our ability to endure, or even to suffer. SAS selection is hard, physically demanding and goes on for six months, but it is the ability to keep going when you are cold, tired, wet and hungry that makes us what we are. Resilience is a superpower. It can trump most natural ability just through hard work and dedication. It can defeat something stronger through heart, desire and the ability to not give up. It can even improve your physical being by thinking more positively. Resilience has always helped me but it can help you too. Resilience is in us all. Cast your mind back to when you were only around six months old and learning to walk. You probably didn't smash it first time, in fact, you probably fell over. Not just once or twice but countless times, perhaps even hundreds of times. But you kept trying, you got up, dusted yourself off and you tried again. Not dissuaded by failure, or embarrassed that you had failed, or whether anyone was watching you. You didn't even know for certain that you could walk. But you kept going and eventually you walked. Then you walked a bit further and maybe even a bit faster but 'always a little bit further'.

That tells me that we are all born with a certain, not insignificant, amount of resilience. How many times do we try something and fail, fall flat on our faces and, unfazed, just get up and try again? Not many. Something happens to us on our journey. We are products of our environment and experiences and that either depletes or adds to the resilience tanks that we are all born with. Sometimes, going through something difficult or even traumatic can strengthen our resolve – but it can also weaken it. History tells us that the someone who wasn't perhaps as gifted as the other person can still overcome through hard work, determination, attitude and, essentially, resilience. On Special Forces selection, I wasn't the biggest, strongest, fastest or fittest, but I had the ability to keep going. I could keep going even when others around me faltered, doubted, failed at something and gave up. Of course, it's more than just a stubborn refusal to quit. It's the ability to believe in yourself and know that even if you can't do something now, you can improve. It's the ability not to be put off by rejection or failure. Not to be perturbed by someone saying you can't or it's not possible. We can shape our own destiny. This was just my next chapter and I was going to need resilience for that too.

* * *

The military has changed a lot over the years. People tell me now you can grow beards, and at the depot recruits can give instructors yellow cards if they feel anxious about language or physical exertions they are put through. This means the instructor has to effectively 'back off'. If not, then the recruit can issue a red card, and the instructor can potentially be RTU'd back to his or her unit! This does seem absurd, and I feel like it can't be true and if so, then what kind of soldier are we creating? One that can endure? Suffer? Go the extra mile? Survive behind enemy lines and withstand interrogations? Probably not, but it's the world we seem to be in at the moment. Rightly or wrongly but it makes me sad in a way and I think perhaps the elite part of what our military used to be is eroding away slowly.

COMPLETING THE CIRCUIT

The first insurgent seemed to come from nowhere.

Black clothes, gloves and a sinister-looking balaclava. 'This guy thinks he's SAS', I thought, but it would turn out that he thought he was Superman, or some close relation.

If he was looking for a fancy-dress party he had come to the wrong place. It was 3.00 am. My breath was clouding as it hit the cold night air, and I moved forward ready to block this sudden intruder's progress. Then I saw the rest of them: more black figures silhouetted by the beam from my torch.

'We've got trouble here', I told Dekka, who had just returned from a quick check of the perimeter. The first couple of guys were armed with ropes and hooks, and behind them came more guys with ladders. They weren't exactly stealthy, but they were clearly determined.

'If they make it over the fence and into the compound we're in the shit', I thought. Time to radio for backup, and then, with a couple more strides, I was in the face of Mr Balaclava.

'This is a restricted area and...' I started, but he ignored me and tried to push past.

Dekka got to the next one as he darted behind me, but the others were already clambering up the fence. 'Shit! How many of these guys are there?' I wondered. We were seriously outnumbered.

Desperate they might have been, but they were not the superheroes they thought they were, and we had air support on the way.

It was January 2005 and, working with a mate's private security company, I was tasked with guarding Channel 4's *Celebrity Big*

Brother compound at Elstree Studios, north of London. Inside, oblivious to the tussles going on beyond their walls, the likes of Bez, Caprice, Brigitte Nielsen and John McCririck were doing whatever it was they were doing in the *Celebrity Big Brother* house.

Our 'attackers', we learned, were protesters from the Fathers4Justice campaign group. Thirteen men and two women, they had planned to climb on to the roof of the *Celebrity Big Brother* house and drop food supplies into the compound for the celebrity contestants 'to raise awareness of the lack of men's rights to see their children'. I had no argument with their cause, but they weren't getting in, not on my watch.

But stopping them wouldn't be easy. Never mind Jackie Stallone inside; we could have done with her son Sylvester out here with us, as, thwarted in their attempts to get on to the roof, the protesters threw fireworks instead. Dekka and I had to literally fight them and try to disarm them until the cavalry arrived. Luckily, they weren't long in coming. Twelve police officers rushed to the scene in answer to our radio call, and a police helicopter with heat-seeking equipment was soon hovering overhead to help them round up the would-be invaders in the dark.

At least the Fathers4Justice founder Matt O'Connor did our references no harm when he told the press why his members had launched their raid and how they had been foiled, describing security at the compound as 'a damn sight tighter than at Buckingham Palace'.

Rewind a bit, and the last couple of years had taken its toll on D Squadron. Four or five guys had already left, and after I signed off another four followed, almost all of them from around the same era as me. That left a huge generation gap, as seven guys had died due to accidents and one had been killed on operation. The squadron would soon lose yet another man, my friend with whom I'd done my hospital attachment. He was shot and killed during an operation in the Middle East, doing the same job that I had. One more name to add to the clock.

I was fortunate that some of my friends were already employed in the security industry, otherwise known as 'the circuit', and were working in Baghdad. I applied to join them and was soon employed as a security consultant protecting the media, among others. I had four other ex-D Squadron guys around me within the team, and we had armoured cars, proper weapons and tracking beacons; we also had a QRF in the shape of the US military less than ten minutes away in case of emergency or to casevac any injuries.

The pay was obviously better and I got more time off, which I spent mostly travelling, and because of this I didn't pay the heavy taxes we faced in the military, even when we were on ops for six months at a time. I was involved in one of the biggest triple car bombings in history by being in the middle of the famous roundabout in Baghdad where Saddam's statue was pulled down. Three different truck bombs flew past me in different directions, the last one a cement mixer full of explosives, and they each detonated all around me, leaving me and the bureau chief completely unscathed inside!

After seeing how the circuit worked, I designed my own security website and became joint director of the company with a friend, though we lacked the commercial and business savvy to keep it going for too long. While it lasted, I looked after the Saudi royal family and many A-list celebrities and high-ranking politicians. That CP (close protection) training in the regiment was starting to pay off.

Apart from guarding celebrities at MTV and in the *Celebrity Big Brother* house, I looked after Tony Blair and Gordon Brown during their trips to Baghdad whilst on the circuit. We were working alongside their Special Branch bodyguards, but British police took something of a back seat in places like Iraq and Afghanistan, accepting the local knowledge of us guys on the ground, and only fully taking the reins again at the airport on the way out.

The best part of the job, by far, was bodyguarding the media, not least because I had taken a fancy to one of the correspondents, a Kuwaiti girl called Kianne. I had seen Kianne at a barbecue when the American NBC News crew I was working for invited CNN staff to their villa in Baghdad, and I thought she looked lovely. When she turned up a month later working for NBC I was immediately drawn to her warm and sociable personality ... and even her more fiery side!

The bodyguard-client relationship is a bit clichéd as an image, but when you're living beside people in the thick of the fighting you become embedded in their lives, and you get to know them very well, very quickly. We grew close after I became her favourite. She would always ask for me to guard her on jobs or trips she was going on, and we flirted for a while, but we never made more of it during the task. It was still a very professional relationship.

That was until we were both working in Germany during the 2006 football World Cup, where she was reporting for NBC and I was initially looking after the Saudi royal family, and we became an item. By the time we were back in Iraq we made no secret of the fact that we were together. Some of the guys frowned upon it, as that kind of relationship is a big no-no in the bodyguarding game, but I couldn't really help it.

Not that it was straightforward bodyguarding Kianne anyway. She would never wear her body armour, and we had big fights about it, so I thought, 'I'll marry her and then she might do what I tell her.' Of course, that didn't work out, but we soon had two beautiful children, Darius and Skye.

However, the circuit was not exciting me, and I'd saved up some money by then, so we decided that I would go to university. Having being told my whole army life that, armed with my little red book of army experience, anyone would welcome me with open arms, I was surprised when The University of Edinburgh told me I would need to go to college before I could be accepted for a degree.

I was disappointed at first, but thought, 'OK, if that's what I've got to do to get where I want to go, then so be it.'

The trouble was that even getting to that stage wasn't going to be easy, and four Edinburgh-based colleges rejected me before I finally managed to secure a place at Newbattle Abbey College. Their motto was *Sero Sed Serio,* which translated from Latin meant 'Late but in earnest' and seemed a perfect fit. So, this was selection, education-style, eh? Well, if at first you don't … As I had previously shown in the military, I would not give up.

When I finally got to do them, the extra studies were great. I got to dip my toe into many different subjects, and particularly enjoyed both history and philosophy. Having been rejected by the other colleges, I studied twenty subjects in total at Newbattle … and got twenty A's. I was thrilled and applied to three universities – and got rejected by them all. Rejection is one of those things that can either break us or mould our resolve and I had seen that the colleges who had all rejected me may well have been the ones at fault not me so I fought and managed to secure a place at the University of Edinburgh to study history.

As I was back home and able to spend a bit more time with my brother and sisters, it became apparent that my brother John was having difficulties. It was clear to me that his severe learning difficulties were something along the lines of Asperger's or autism. He had managed to maintain a job and had his own flat, but things were not going well. I went around to see him at his flat and it was knee-deep in rubbish throughout and he was struggling with work and stuff so I took him out of his environment and moved him in with me and tried to help him. Of course, I was the last person he was going to let help as I was the big brother who was away with the army and he found it difficult to let me help.

I was able to help so many other people but was really struggling to help my own brother and in desperation I went to visit my mother, who I hadn't really spoken with since leaving for the army as a boy. I knocked on her door and she initially didn't recognise me but when I told her my concerns for John she played it down and said it wasn't as serious as I was saying. I left completely shocked and disappointed. A week later, John completed suicide.

He had been a troubled soul, and I was already deeply dismayed by the failure to get John medically diagnosed.

He had gone missing, and I spent a desperate week trying to find him during daylight hours. My feeling of helplessness was only intensified by the police, who came to the house and suggested that I was lying about having been in the SAS, and that perhaps I had beaten John up because I was embarrassed that he was gay. I couldn't fathom why they were pursuing such lines of enquiry, not least because, as far as I knew, John wasn't gay. I managed to contain myself and threw them out of the house.

My misery was complete when John's body was found. Seeing my SAS comrades dead had been bad enough, but identifying my brother's body after he had deliberately drowned himself and lain undiscovered for a week was a whole new level of pain.

I miss him dearly to this day, but I know that he is in a better place now. The loss of my brother drew me not only closer still to my sisters, but also to my stepfather, who took it very badly. I'd already lost all patience with my mother for what I regarded as her lack of concern over what John was suffering, but my stepdad was different.

For all his faults, he was a kind and generous man and had no airs and graces. He would give me the last pound in his pocket, and I was convinced that when he hit me as a child he always resented doing so. That's why I was pleased that we were able to reconcile and that I had something of a relationship with him. In the wake of John's death, I immersed myself in books, and found myself thoroughly enjoying my university history course, particularly the British history I was studying. My tutor and dissertation coach throughout this period was Dr Alex Murdoch, whose character, method of teaching and knowledge were a revelation to me. I was also fortunate enough to work with people like Professor Tom Devine, Jenny Wormald and Gordon Pentland.

University was tough, and made all the tougher because, of course, I had two young children at the time, and I often commuted down to London to take over the care of Darius and Skye while Kianne worked shifts, and then I would take the sleeper back up to Edinburgh for my studies. Those were hard times, and the sleep deprivation was probably on a par with what I went through during selection! I also needed to earn some money, so I applied for a number of jobs and again faced blanket rejection. Over the course of a year, I applied for over a thousand jobs without a single interview. I started high and aimed at middle management, until eventually a year later I applied for a role as a night shift security guard at the National Library of Scotland, which I had thought might work well with my university studies. To my dismay, I was rejected again with the opening line reading 'Unfortunately, due to the overwhelming calibre of applicants you have not been selected for interview ...' I kept that letter and still have it to this day to remind me of where I am now and where I could have found myself. I've always tried to remain humble and grounded and never thought I was deserving of anything more than what I had worked for. It has stood me in good stead, and any time I feel low or think I need a boost, I look at that letter and remind myself how lucky I am to have things that are important.

After a year of rejections, I found myself ambling down the Royal Mile in Edinburgh and a young man asked if I wanted to buy the *Big Issue*. I bought one, thinking it would soon be me there selling it the way things were going, and on the back page I noticed a volunteer role advertised. It was for a project worker role and the organisation was Cyrenians. The theme of the role was conflict resolution and the irony of the theme wasn't lost on me so I thought *sod it ... I'll apply* and was amazed to receive an email back inviting me for an interview! I went along to the interview in front of a panel of three women and was asked, 'Colin, tell us about a time you successfully resolved a conflict.' I walked out of there about an hour later, perhaps after giving them all PTSD; when they called me back and said I had got the job, I felt very smug with myself! I was gobsmacked. I went along to Cyrenians and found out that the role involved going into secondary schools in Central Scotland and teaching conflict resolution where it was needed.

Cyrenians had just won the project funding and had no material and it was on me to research the topic and create the programme. I started with a fresh slate and went into schools and to my surprise found a lot of success, pupils were staying in school and conflict was reduced. Eventually the independent schools got wind of it and asked me to come along and that they would make a contribution to Cyrenians. Then the Prince's Trust heard and asked if they could shadow me on one of my courses and put my course as part of the year-long XL programme, which is run up and down the UK. From being unemployable in my mind, I had created something life-changing, which was being rolled out across the UK. A lot of people have said that I should be proud to have helped so many children and, in some cases, may have saved their lives, but the opposite is true. At a time when I was low and didn't know if I was going to find my way on this planet, they saved me. Of that, there's no doubt. We are always just a circumstance or choice away from being at our lowest or highest. I've never forgotten that.

I took on a number of part-time jobs. The first was general TV extra work. I was a regular extra in the TV detective series *Taggart* and *River City*, and I had a few speaking parts on the BBC *A History of Scotland* series. This gave me my first real taste for TV – not including my brush with *Soldier Soldier* or *Gladiators* – and I loved it. I also did some minor modelling, holding whisky glasses or drills, but I quickly grew sick of people phoning to ask if I was available at the weekend for a hand job! On one particular day I was asked to model for an NHS campaign, so I went down to a basement in Leith, happy to help the health service I had briefly worked with during my SAS medic's course. That was until they told me what they wanted me to do. They asked if I would be prepared to strip naked and lie face down on a bed for a photo as part of their campaign to warn of the dangers of HIV and to promote the use of protection.

It was undoubtedly for a great cause, but I was not happy. Who would be? I refused, but they insisted that they would blur my face, so I agreed. To my horror, my face was not only *not* blurred, but blown up poster size, and the photos appeared across every GP surgery and toilet wall in Central Scotland! I still get people mentioning seeing it to this day.

While I was doing the TV extra work I was looked up by one of the staff from Rockstar Games, the people who make worldwide hit video games like *Grand Theft Auto*, *Max Payne*, *Red Dead Redemption*, *L.A. Noire* and others, and she asked me, 'Would you do mocap?' 'Would I do what?' I asked. It sounded like another NHS con to me, but she explained that it was motion capture, the sort of stuff that Andy Serkis famously did as the character Gollum in the *Lord of the Rings* movie series, but for video games, not feature films.

Essentially, it meant dressing up in a Lycra suit covered in sensors and being filmed doing movements such as wielding weapons or throwing someone onto a mat. They capture the movement and translate it into the graphics for their video games. It's great fun, a really relaxed but professional work ethic, and I've seen Rockstar North grow in size, stature and capabilities over the years that I've been working there. Francesca first recruited me, and later Simon took over in the Motion Capture seat and if you're a gamer you may well be familiar with the likes of detective-turned-vigilante-turned-bodyguard Max Payne; and you'll probably know of retired bank robber Michael De Santa, his ex-Repo man sidekick Franklin Clinton, and mentally unstable redneck Trevor Phillips, all from *Grand Theft Auto*. You may also know *Red Dead Redemption* protagonist John Marston, the son of a prostitute, who had a difficult childhood with a flawed dad and went into care before living the life of a gun-toting outlaw with a strict moral code. If they wield a weapon or get into a fight, it may not be my face you see on screen, but it may be my moves they make. Although there is an uncanny resemblance between Arthur Morgan and me and we haven't been seen in the same room…

Meanwhile, the time that Dr Murdoch and others at the University of Edinburgh invested in me must have paid off, because I emerged with a First-Class MA (Hons) in history and was the first student to win all three prizes for both best student, best in history and best dissertation. I was also runner up in the national undergraduate of the year awards. It just went to show that, despite not finishing school, I could still achieve at the highest academic level. This was the same student who was rejected countless times from colleges and universities for not being regarded as 'good enough'. Remember that the next time someone 'judges' you or makes a decision on you. It is sometimes as much a reflection of them as you.

I was never the smartest person at university but I learned the game and outworked the competition. You can do that at almost anything, whether it's playing an instrument, learning a language, playing a sport or practising a skill. I nearly failed my very first essay. I still remember now, I had to answer the question 'Was Scotland ever conquered?', I answered 'no', and then described all the evidence and reasons why. It was then I discovered that under these 'rules of the game' at university I had only half answered the question and hadn't described all the reasons why they *were* conquered. I learned fast and then simply outworked the rest of the class. When there was an essay I would set aside time and stick to it rigidly. I would practice any given essay or exam at least a dozen times before I sat it for real. Then when it came to attempting it for real not only did I know what I was going to write, I could tell you almost to the letter how many words I was going to write in that time. It was just a case of how quickly I could write to fill the time.

The military prepares you for all that. Train for real. Use all the time preparing for that small time when you are in the arena. Marginal gains are crucial. Work for every point. Learn, practice, improve and repeat. Few things had priority over preparing for these exams and essays and the results showed that. More often than not, you get out what you put in. There were plenty of kids more naturally gifted than me for education. They had better memory retention, natural subject knowledge, more resources. A better prior education. I just outworked them. And so can you.

Not content with that, however, I also studied Terrorism at University of St Andrews, and still edit articles for them now, and I wrote a chapter in a counter-insurgency publication. I've always been keen on learning and reading, particularly when it pertains to history or Scotland or military, or even The Enlightenment, which was the subject of my dissertation. After graduating, I applied to a management-consultancy firm, but the process took forever, and while I was waiting for a partner interview an opportunity came up working for a risk-management consultancy, mainly for oil and gas clients. It was a great job, I made some good friends, and during this time I was invited to get involved in a TV series putting ordinary people through SAS-style selection challenges.

Setting goals for yourself is so important. If you don't believe me, try it. Write down three goals. They can be big, medium and short, or long term and short term. Whatever works for you, but when you make them you are more inclined to stick to them. You also see that on days you don't think you are making any progress that actually by checking in with small goals you are making a step forward and not a step back. A step closer to your main goal.

FROM SHADOWS TO
THE LIMELIGHT

Just a few years after working for Channel 4 as a security guard (consultant), I would now be working for them in front of the camera in the show *SAS: Who Dares Wins*. At the time we didn't think it would be as successful as it was, but it gave me another insight into the world of television, and I loved it. I was the first and only SAS guy to be put in the team and the rest of the guys were SBS (Special Boat Service). We had to get EPAW to take part and everything was signed off by the MOD. I didn't know any of the other guys during my service time but they knew each other. The production company had told us that they would stay out of it and we could run it ourselves and they would only interfere to change batteries or cameras etc. That wasn't quite true and I was surprised when, after we had just agreed as a DS team on which few candidates we were going to let go, the production team intercepted us and asked us to change our minds as one was homosexual and one was of an ethnic minority. I couldn't believe it, but we grudgingly changed the people we had agreed upon. It always stuck with me as being ethically wrong and not something that wouldn't have even entered the conversation at Hereford.

They may well have been keen to avoid being viewed as homophobic or racist, but in acting in that way they were being just as biased. In a separate example, one of the candidates who had taken his armband off and essentially 'VW'd was requested to come back as it made good TV. These sorts of things are not aligned with how it worked on SAS selection. Of course, it was hard work too, and while at one stage during the interrogation phase the contestants were allowed to get some sleep and a hot drink, nobody seemed to give a thought to the ex-SF guys, and we got less sleep than the candidates! Not that I wasn't used to sleep deprivation, of course. Selection is always a fine line between training and preparing people for as close to the real thing and keeping them safe, and while we always err on the side of caution there have been times when we have lost candidates on UKSF selection. We maintain that we could make it 'easier' or take more responsibility away from the candidates, but the reality is we would only increase their risk if and when they find themselves behind enemy lines and we want to give them the best chance of success.

People always ask how 'real' the show is, or how much like the real SAS selection it is. For example, could any of the candidates who get to the end of the show successfully make it through the real SAS selection and obviously it's a resounding no from me. Anything else would be a disservice to our servicemen and women who have tried and failed the process, many of them after decades of military service. To think someone off the street could just rock up and smash SAS selection is absurd. For a start, the infanteer side of soldiering is not there, which is a really critical part of the process, particularly for phases like the jungle. Then we have to consider how long they are on the test for. On the show we had the candidates for around eight days, whereas selection is relentless for six months!

That said, I liked the real and gritty aspect of the earlier series. They got ordinary, real people and put them in extraordinary situations and showed the public what they could do. I liked that aspect and wish they would have stuck with this rather than follow the typical reality TV format of chasing a backstory or getting celebrities involved. Once people like Katie Price were involved I knew the show had gone downhill; ordinary people don't relate as much to celebrities, we identify more with people who have similar attributes, fears, strengths etc. I also didn't like how the show seemed to amplify the swearing and shouting side of selection, which really doesn't exist. The motivation has to come from yourself, not some DS swearing and shouting at you. Then there is the introduction of Americans, and it all just tends to go a bit Hollywood.

I'm glad I was involved when I was because I liked the concept of the show and it started out quite honest and gritty. Many people have asked why I came out of the shadows or appeared on television when we are supposed to remain secret and there are those out there who strongly disagree with it, but I guess the proof is in the pudding. Does the good of coming out of the shadows outweigh the bad? Generally I think it does. It is good for your profile if you are trying to raise it for yourself or for good causes etc. It is good for the public to know (within reason) what goes on and what kind of people are out there looking after us and good for them to hopefully help conquer fears or get them interested in getting fit, going outdoors or improving mental health. Finally, I think things like this are good for recruitment. Movies like *Top Gun* increased the number of candidates applying to be fighter jet pilots.

The same argument could be made when we recall Operation Nimrod, the mission where the SAS first revealed themselves to members of the UK public through their TV sets in 1980 in the storming of the Iranian Embassy in London. It's no coincidence that showing the world what the UK's stance was on terrorism and what they would throw against it led to the lack of terrorist incidents on UK mainland for a long time afterwards when it was rising quickly throughout the majority of the rest of Europe. Shows more recently like *SAS: Rogue Heroes*, while not completely accurate, serve to show how we started and why we need these people to protect our shores. Some things are useful for the public to see and know, and other things are best not known. I would estimate, based on my own to date assesment, that there are probably around fifty counter-terror operations within the UK every year. That's about one a week. I would also estimate that places like GCHQ can only monitor so many people at any one time so it stands to reason that every now and then one will slip through the net but for the majority of the time good people are doing what they can to keep Britain safe.

After that, I was interviewed by the BBC and ITN on the political issue of the Chilcot Report, which looked at the justification for war, and quite soon afterwards, I was in a Channel 5 series, *Secrets of the SAS*. Sadly, as the TV work went well my marriage to Kianne was suffering. I moved to take up a job in Kuwait, Kianne's homeland, wondering if I might feel differently there about our marriage, which had been flat for a couple of years, but sadly it didn't work out. I made the difficult decision to commence divorce proceedings, knowing that my children would be in Kuwait while I returned to the UK. I realised that our children would be happier if their parents were happier, so I was determined to make a clean break and return to my homeland to make the TV career work and throw myself into charity work whenever possible. Sometimes in life, the more success and happiness you get, the bigger the fall you experience, and despite all the scrapes I had got into and low points I had experienced, the next one was to prove the lowest I had ever experienced and the closest I have ever come to contemplating suicide.

On one of my visits back to the UK just prior to returning permanently, I was pitching a spy series to the Discovery Channel and had a meeting with their guys in London. This was a separate project and team to the Channel 4 team and I had in place a TV agent and a book agent. I was also pitching the very manuscript you are reading to a book publisher after initially getting what seemed like a green light from the MOD disclosure cell. I also had a few other projects, sponsorship deals and opportunities including the next series of *SAS: Who Dares Wins* in the pipeline and everything looked good. The very night we had done our meeting with the Discovery Channel I met a woman. Eager to embrace my single life after a failed marriage and thinking things had gone well, I walked with her to the station the following morning before flying back to Kuwait to finally pack up and make arrangements to move home to the UK.

By the time I arrived in Kuwait she had messaged my ex-wife and was acting completely irrationally. I told her I didn't want to speak to her and she started attacking people online and anyone she thought had a connection with me. I flew home and her behaviour was getting worse and she was now stalking me to the point where I had to get the police involved. At one stage, she had called me fifty-two times in an hour! She would text and lie that she was pregnant, and then she would text and say she would kill herself if I didn't call, and then when I did she laughed and said she would never do that. Because my brother had taken his own life, this enraged me. I texted her back some choice words of which I'm not proud; she had caught me at a bad time and on a topic I feel passionately about.

The police got involved and things became very stressful for a while. At this time, I lived in Scotland and the woman in question lived in England, which complicated matters legally. Any alleged crime she might have committed with her communications had to be dealt with under English Law, so the Scottish police couldn't interview her and had no power to enforce anything. Fortunately, this seemed to be enough to stop the harassment for a while.

At around this time, several things were happening. As mentioned, the TV agent cancelled our contract. The book agent and publisher cancelled theirs. The Discovery Channel project team dropped me, and all the guys from the Channel 4 show just went radio silence on me. I reached out to Ant Middleton and he said he wouldn't do another show without me. This sounded reassuring as I had always wanted to make sure our strength on the show was as a team. I had provisionally tried to write into my contract that no one would get paid less than me and no one would get paid more. I didn't want to see us used against each other or discarded as pawns. They had promised us retainers as long as we only worked with them and no other channel, but I was concerned there was never going to be enough work for us all and perhaps one person would be promoted at the expense of everyone else. I didn't want to see us picked off individually and discarded and a new flavour brought in when they got bored with us. I got on with most of the guys on the show and I put Channel 4 in touch with Billy Billingham as he's a top bloke and I served with him in the same troop. Jason Fox is a decent guy too, but Ant and I have very different values and ethics and we are different people. That's fine, Special Forces are full of different people, but I have a long successful military career and friends I have built over a lifetime who know what I stand for.

I was still sleeping on my stepdad's couch with no work lined up; I took a visit to South Queensferry. A beautiful quaint town on the outskirts of Edinburgh and walked across the famous Forth Road Bridge. The sun was shining and I felt really tired of several nights with little or no sleep. I let thoughts enter my head. I wondered if the world would be better off without me. Would anyone miss me? Everyone could stop the attacks, or would they just turn on someone else. I realised how small the world is when these things happen. How true friends stand beside you and don't desert you in your time of need. I looked over the edge and wondered how long it would take me to fall. I probably wouldn't feel anything and maybe people would just think I had disappeared. Then I thought about my children, Darius and Skye. I knew how much it hurt when my brother John had completed suicide and having to identify him when he had drowned. I wouldn't want that for anyone and I slowly walked back home.

Darius and Skye were not my only children. When I was really young, perhaps 19 or 20, I went out with a girl for a short while and we split up, but she had a baby and her name was Sarah. I had no idea at the time and my mother had tried to keep it from me but many years later, when Sarah was only around 13, she reached out on Facebook and we met up. Like a lot of things, I tried to throw myself into it but it wasn't to be at that time and we drifted a bit. She was bright and quick witted and had my sense of humour and I know she will do well in life. Children have always been part of my life and sometimes, when we have a particularly bad or traumatic childhood, we try and make sure we improve others.

Our journey in life is often intertwined with crossroads. Small moments in the duration of our lifetime but taking one turn leads you along one path while the other leads a different way. I met a woman at this time who not only lifted me almost singlehandedly out from my abyss, but enabled me to become the best version of myself and showcase the good qualities I had. Amanda and I had a mutual friend from my military days and from the day we met it seemed just natural that we should spend the rest of our lives together. She was beautiful, kind and had a fierceness about her which I admired. Of course, I should have known as our paths had crossed many times before we met romantically!

We had been seeing each other for maybe a year or so when I casually remarked about moving to stay in Livingston for a small time when I was very young. Amanda looked at me quizzingly 'whereabout in Livingston?' she asked. 'Oh Larchbank' I replied. 'I used to go to the nursery there', and she looked at me bewildered. It turned out we stayed about a dozen houses apart and went to the same nursery at the same time! Moreover, I also found out that when I had been working for Cyrenians, she had worked across the road at Hibernian Football Club and we had shared the same car park. It's funny how we have those sliding doors moments and I'm glad she found me. We all need to be rescued occasionally. Our stars aligned and she is not only the love of my life but my best friend. Many years later we found an old school picture from primary one – I could see Amanda and where was I standing? Right behind her! It was surreal and a little scary, but we love that our lives were that close and that we drew back to each other many years later. The world can be a small place sometimes.

I got involved in public speaking completely by chance. I was working in an oil and gas role in Aberdeen around 2014, where I was teaching emergency response for any potential future Piper Alpha incidents when an annual conference for the sector was due to be held. The theme for the conference was risk and we were supposed to have this skydiver parachute in and talk to everyone on risk, but he cancelled the day before so everyone was in a flap. I mentioned to the organisers that I could step in and talk if they were desperate but it would have a military angle on things. They must have been desperate as they agreed and I went up on this stage at the Aberdeen Conference Centre to a couple of hundred people and did my talk. I got a standing ovation and a woman approached me and asked how long I had been a speaker and was amazed when I replied with 'about an hour'.

She said she worked in events and that I should do more public speaking, so I started on just one website initially and then, as word of mouth and reputation grew, ended up on around 20 speaking platforms and I've done over 500 talks to date. I really enjoy them and you get to travel around meeting different people and organisations. I have a lot of repeat clients and I always tailor my talks around what the theme is they are striving for, such as teamwork, leadership, resilience or elite performance. I would like to mention my old tour manager, Gaenor, who sadly passed with cancer in 2022. We had plans for a UK-wide speaking tour which sadly was cut short, but I wanted her to see this come to fruition as she worked hard at all the events she organised. People can quite often forget the people around them who have helped them get where they are, particularly as they get higher, but I never forget people who have helped me regardless of where I was. It's probably poignant to mention my friend Rab who helped me out quite a bit when I was having difficulties. Rab owns a gym in Edinburgh and has helped me with various issues since leaving the SAS, volunteering to give up many hours of his time. It's easy for friends to stand by you when you're doing well, but when you're low and it feels like world is attacking you, then only the great friends stand beside you and share that fight. We remember those who helped us when we were in a time of need and not just when we were flying high.

That also got me involved in my teamwork and leadership workshops, which I do all over the country and these can be anything from a half day to a two-year long company-wide initiative. I love these and they are always a mix of talks, spreadsheets, fun exercises and problems and activities and I believe in mixing up the different learning styles to keep it fresh and engaging while throwing in exciting tales and anecdotes along the way! It's taken me around Europe and the United States and I get to meet really diverse and interesting people and organisations.

Sometimes they want military style activities run or they may want a fun day where their CEO is kidnapped and then they are launched on a problem-solving mission to rescue them. Occasionally, it will involve tapping into different modules pertaining to management or leadership where I come in once a quarter and talk about something like decision making, leadership styles, conflict resolution or motivating teams etc. I have always been more interested in motivating corporates and the cognitive style of Special Forces, as opposed to any fitness or physical attributes. I wouldn't be motivated by a business that centres around shouting at people to do more press ups or run faster. That's why, in my workshops or doing one of my Stoic Events, we always focus on the mindset and the cognitive side of things involving problems, challenges or code breaking etc. If you want to know any more about either talks, workshops or Stoic Events you can check it out on my website at www.colin22sas.com.

Facing rejection and criticism has been a major part of my life. I will always be disappointed with other people's actions and trying to reconcile it in my mind. With experience, we come to embrace rejection and failure better and realise it can quite often be a reflection of the 'other person' and not us. Bear that in mind.

'Worrying does not take away tomorrow's troubles.
It takes always today's peace.'

Randy Armstrong

TO BE A PILGRIM

No story of mine would be complete without mentioning the great charities and projects I am proud to be associated with. I think we all have a certain obligation to 'give back' as and when we can. Some charities I have been working with for over a decade and some maybe four or five years. I don't mention those for whom I have done one-off stuff, as I think we all do that naturally anyway, but those that I have a long-standing relationship with.

The NSPCC will seem a fairly obvious link and I have done bits and bobs with them for over a decade. Mostly fund raisers and raising awareness but I was most fortunate to go out to Nepal following the earthquakes in 2016 to help rebuild schools as part of the Worldwide Action Group and helped raise a significant amount for NSPCC. It was also quite heart-warming to see children as young as 10 walk several miles to learn how to construct these buildings and then walk back to their communities to help them build theirs. Can you imagine that in the UK? I have fond memories of running back down the mountain, which took the best part of an hour but will without doubt be the most beautiful run I have ever taken. Running through the green covered mountains as the sun was rising stopping only to grab a drink from a small waterfall or stream. Life can be great sometimes in its raw and primitive form. Even when people have very little in terms of wealth, possessions or education they can be as happy if more so than a millionaire. Again, we are products of our environment and sometimes people today gaze at social media to see what their lives 'should' look like or what a role model is and that can sometimes be a really poor example.

I'm also a panel member and qualified chair for the Children's Panel in Scotland. I give a couple of days per month to sit on children's hearings and decide on best outcomes for children dependant on their circumstances. Having been on the other side of the Children's Panel I can empathise with the children sat across from me and I like to think my actions have had positive outcomes for them all. I've always thought the best people to deal with anyone who has come through trauma is someone who has walked a mile in their shoes and speaks the same language. This is true not only for children but veterans and ex-firefighters, police, ambulance service, prison wardens and NHS etc. I remember it being a scary thing, sat across from three strangers explaining the intimate details of my life at that age; I try to use that memory to inform how I come across at meetings. We can all use the bad examples in our life as guidance for what not to do in our own actions.

I am also passionate about our Armed Forces and particularly our veterans. It is my honest opinion that nobody in society gives more than our military. In terms of risk to their lives, time spent away from family and the sacrifices and hard work they display, there are few professions that *give* as much. It's not particularly well paid either so I think HM Forces owe a debt to our veterans when they leave to ensure they have the basics: a roof over their head, safety, food and a basic quality of life. Most of all just a decent chance to have a successful life after the military and I've always thought that's the least you should expect when you sacrifice so much.

In my opinion there shouldn't have to be so many private charities relying on grants and funding. There should just be one Armed Forces charity that looks after everyone but of course life isn't simple and there are so many military charities now. I became a patron/ambassador for both the Pilgrim Bandits and Lee Rigby Foundation back around 2016. Pilgrim Bandits were doing great stuff with amputees and their services now encompass a far wider group of veterans. They do many things and have taken veterans on some brilliant expeditions and gruelling endurance events to show that the mindset of veterans allows them to achieve far more beyond simply what their limbs can allow.

The Lee Rigby Foundation was set up by Lee's mother Lyn after the horrific execution of Lee on the streets of the UK. I have done speaking events for them at fundraisers, raised awareness through projects and even donned a Rangers top to play alongside the Rangers legends of the past such as Mols, Laudrup, Wallace and Gascoigne, with Mark Hateley as their manager. I have to say few football clubs in Britain do more for our Armed Forces than Rangers and they were always brilliant with me regardless of my football allegiances. I am a Celtic supporter even though most of my friends are Rangers fans, but I've never been one of those Celtic fans that has hated Rangers – being ex-Special Forces you gather a respect for your opponent and even I can see that for both clubs, and Scottish football in general, both teams have to improve and be better, to push each other to be better. I always want Rangers to do well in European competition and I've donned more Rangers tops on for charity than I ever have for Celtic. In Scotland, football, religion, politics and sectarianism are closely linked and it can be too easy to be identified with one and then put in a silo and treated accordingly. It's funny how rugby is so different. I enjoy going to the rugby as well and it's amazing how rugby fans are mixed and, win, lose or draw, are not drawn into violence. Of course, a lot of this stems from how the players conduct themselves on to the pitch, as role models for the fans. You have 20-stone, muscle-strewn men listening patiently to the referee and calling him sir with a genuine respect for the rules and the game. That's how life should be played out. Imagine a world where opposing football fans sat side by side and – win, lose or draw – shook hands and went home or out for a drink with the opposition.

Another charity based in Scotland that I worked with until 2023 was Ancre Somme Association Scotland. ASA Scotland was formed to keep the memory alive of those that were lost during both world wars and after. They do lots of work going into schools, educating on former pupils who went on to do heroic acts, or were lost during conflict. They then often make a bench or memorial garden at the school. This is great, as sometimes the history behind our wars is left out of the school curriculum. They also raise money for memorials and cairns, and I was proud to be part of the John McAleese memorial and the cairn for David Penman, both of whom I had met. I stepped away from the charity in 2023 due to issues with the management.

I formed Who Dares Cares alongside a friend called Calum MacLeod back in 2016 as we both recognised that there was no 24/7 support available for veterans and that if a veteran was struggling and reaching out, then sometimes, they couldn't wait days, weeks or months for an appointment or to speak to someone. They needed someone now. So we created WDC with a view to having a social group that could lean on each other and they do events such as our walk, talk and brew events, which have spread from just being in the central belt of Scotland to little regional hubs all over. We also wanted to create an app that provided round the clock coverage, which would put a service user in contact immediately with a responder who would not only match their details geographically but also from a service background perspective, so they had a better chance of success. With a lot of fund raising and word of mouth we have been successful and helped or saved countless lives thanks to our hard-working volunteers and help from sponsors and also J.P. Morgan, who helped design our app. They do the Kiltwalk, West Highland Way, and many challenges throughout the year. We have no salaries or admin fees and so the money goes where it needs to be. Check out their website or Facebook page out for information and maybe I'll see you at a fundraiser or event!

I took up golf fairly late on in life and have met some great friends around it. There are a few good golfing organisations and charities out there representing veterans, disabled and many others so I thought I would give them a mention and you could check them out.

The On Course Foundation do a lot of good work with our veterans and have a mix of training hubs, work opportunities and great golf days and initiatives like their Simpson Cup named after the founder John Simpson played in a Ryder Cup format between UK and US veteran golfers. The Scottish Disabled Golf and Curling association is also a great group of mixed disabilities, ages and gender, and they also do great golfing events and have their own Phoenix Cup, which competes the UK/Europe against US/Canada and they offer curling as another activity also. Battleback Golf do something similar in the UK and US and there are a number of great initiatives such as the Caddy School for Soldiers where veterans from the UK, US and Canada are retrained as caddies and able to have very successful second careers as caddies.

Amanda organised a trip for me a few years ago. It was to find out who the Maclachlans were and where I had come from. I knew my biological father had died but knew nothing of the rest of my Maclachlan family tree. We travelled through to Oban where I knew he had lived. Traditionally the Clan Maclachlan area was around Loch Fyne, a lovely area of Scotland, so I set out searching for answers. I don't know why we parked up where we did, but we picked a non-descript car park and wandered into a nearby convenience store. The man was friendly and when I asked for directions for the main graveyard as I was trying to trace my father, he pointed me up the hill.

After several hours of scanning gravestones and finding nothing, we ventured back into the main town centre and we wandered into the local museum. I mentioned to the older men behind the counter and they said, 'Aye, Old Peacy Maclachlan'. He had died, but had brothers and a sister, his brother had stayed up at an address near where we had originally parked. When we returned and found the address, a neighbour said that the house's owner was also the owner of the convenience store, so we made our way back in and asked him. 'Peacey Maclachlan was your da?' he exclaimed, and then said,

'My dad and him were best friends.' He locked up the shops and asked us to follow him.

He knocked on his father's door, and when he told him who I was he just stared at me. His wife appeared at the door and the father said, 'Think of the past and tell me whose son you think that is?' His wife said 'Peacey's?', and you could have knocked me over with a feather. They said my father had carried a photo of me around in his wallet until he died and always said it was his regret he never came back for me. They said a few members of the wider family had tried to get in touch but 'a man that was staying at Woolfords answered the phone and said I wasn't interested'. I was devastated. It had obviously been my stepfather, Benny. We met a few other people that had known my father and armed with more answers than I had expected, I drew a line under searching for the rest of my family, at peace with it.

When Covid-19 came along it changed everyone's lives. All of my work ceased overnight. I couldn't do public speaking events or presenter type roles as these events and projects dried up. The motion capture side of things stopped for over two years as well as it's a hard thing to do practically with all the constraints of the virus. I changed my goals and decided to write. I edited my autobiography and renewed my fight to get it cleared. I wrote follow-up books with my spare time on topics such as resilience, public speaking and also a fiction. Sometimes, you have to revisit goals and not be afraid to change them. That's when I co-founded Stoic Events.

It seemed like the whole world wanted to meet up and have fun again and I wanted to create adventures and memories for people. I had access to ranges, weapons, explosives, helicopters, kayaks, military vehicles, POW camps and core team of great staff with interesting and diverse backgrounds and all I did was put the working parts together. We tailor build 'missions' around what companies, sports teams or blue chips tell us and break them into teams for competition. I also like to have a cognitive side of it as opposed to a simply physical side as I wanted it to be fun and capable for literally anyone. I really enjoy it and my team and I may even see you one day at an event.

As I reach the second half of my life I am obviously older, less fit – but far wiser, and would like to think my mental health is better. We only get one shot at life and some things are really important such as your health, family and friends and keeping happy. I've never really been driven by money or wanted to have my ego inflated, but do feel rewarded by some of the charity work I do or quality time I spend with my children, Amanda or my friends. As you go through your life, friends will come and go. Sometimes you don't see how real or close your friends are until you are in a pickle, and then you really see what people are made of. I have learned the hard way in some cases, and I guess I never stop feeling disappointed when one of my 'friends' lets me down or surprises me.

In some ways it hardens our resolve, much the same way as failure does. I have faced rejection so many times and I guess it hardens us to some extent, but it never feels any less painful. I was rejected as a child, rejected occasionally in the army, rejected from colleges and universities and rejected from countless jobs and opportunities. When I look back now though, I succeeded to grow from a child into a man and always remember what true love means to my children. I succeeded in the army where many doubted me and reached the tip of the spear where nobody could deny I was a good soldier. I got into college and made sure I was top and gained entry into university to be the 'First of the Firsts' and take the academic awards. I ended up doing jobs that people said I couldn't. There was a place for me and I made it for myself. When people reject you or tell you that you can't do something just remember that your mindset, determination, attitude and resilience will take you wherever you want it to. It's your superpower, it trumps natural ability and crosses all divides. It has certainly helped me and can help you too.

As I face the future, I hope that I'll continue public speaking, doing motion capture for video games and remaining involved with charities. I would like to be more involved in film and TV, either presenting or acting. I expect there will be more rejection, more failure and more doors slammed in my face. People will let you down but that is life and we can't let that drag us down. We have to focus on our successes and what we can control. Trusting the process and enjoying the moments we have and the memories we create. Keep good people around us and cherish the good friends we have that are there for us when we are at our lowest for those are the truest of friendships. We can build our resilience and throw ourselves out of our comfort zones. We have an inbuilt fear of the unknown or change but when we reflect upon it, most of the fears were just in our head. Think about the last fear you faced, was it as bad as you first thought? Now think about your biggest and proudest achievements, they came with hard work right? Life is one long journey so take every bend and bump and downhill ride as it comes, no matter whatever the surface or weather or how your car looks or feels. You're part of the journey and that's the most important part.

The Special Forces teach you to be committed, determined and driven, though if you want to be a member you pretty much have to be all those things already. We have an inbuilt realisation that, despite adversity, we are survivors. We carry on. I've been abused but come through it; I've been severely challenged but risen to it; I've visited hell and kept on going; I've seen war, and worse, and lived to tell the tale. I've worked with the best of the military world and the intelligence world; I've been a hostage rescuer, hostage negotiator and a hostage; I'm past SAS and currently Max Payne, or Trevor Phillips or Arthur Morgan; but most of all I'm Colin Maclachlan, partner to Amanda my best friend, and dad of Darius and Skye, and they are the centre around which everything else in my life revolves. I love to be with them, and to lavish them with the love and fun that I never received in my childhood. The road has not always been golden, but I'm still on the journey to my Samarkand; still learning, still living and still, hopefully, helping those who need me most.

Such is the life of a pilgrim

※ ※ ※

Finally, an acknowledgement for all my former colleagues, some not with us now and some who are but bear the scars both visible and invisible. And with that I finish with this apt quote,

> It is not the critic who counts; not the man who points out how the strong man stumbles, or where the doer of deeds could have done them better. The credit belongs to the man who is actually in the arena, whose face is marred by dust and sweat and blood; who strives valiantly; who errs, who comes short again and again, because there is no effort without error and shortcoming; but who does actually strive to do the deeds; who knows great enthusiasms, the great devotions; who spends himself in a worthy cause; who at the best knows in the end the triumph of high achievement, and who at the worst, if he fails, at least fails while daring greatly, so that his place shall never be with those cold and timid souls who neither know victory nor defeat.
>
> *Theodore Roosevelt*